The Dinosaur Mindset

The Dinosaur Mindset

Matthew Petchinsky

1

The Dinosaur Mindset: Prehistoric Tactics for Modern Wealth

By: Matthew Petchinsky

Introduction

Survival wasn't optional in the age of dinosaurs—it was strategy. For over 165 million years, apex predators and cunning survivors roamed a world where hesitation meant extinction. Every movement, every choice, was guided by an unyielding instinct to adapt, hunt, and thrive. The weakest were consumed; the strongest carved their legacy into the fossil record. Those lessons did not vanish with the asteroid—they remain etched in our DNA, waiting to be reclaimed.

Today, we live in an environment that looks nothing like the Jurassic swamps or Cretaceous plains. Our predators are no longer fanged reptiles but bills, inflation, competition, and distraction. The prey are not timid herbivores but the millions of people trapped in cycles of financial struggle, moving passively through life without realizing they are being hunted by debt, scarcity, and systems designed to keep them small. The battlefield has shifted, but the game is the same: survive or get devoured.

The difference is this—you are no ordinary prey. Deep within you lies the same primal force that allowed dinosaurs to dominate an unforgiving world. That raw, instinctive mindset can be sharpened into a financial weapon, one powerful enough to cut through modern uncertainty. The rules of prehistoric survival—territory, dominance, resource control, adaptability—are the very strategies that lead to wealth today.

This book is about reclaiming that ferocity. It's not about playing it safe, following the herd, or waiting for permission. It's about seeing yourself as a predator of opportunity, an apex strategist in a world that rewards decisiveness and punishes hesitation. Each chapter uncovers ancient instincts and translates them into practical, modern wealth tactics—showing you how to hunt opportunities, protect your resources, and build an empire that endures.

Dinosaurs didn't survive by luck. They thrived through dominance. And so can you.

Chapter One – Adapt or Die Rich: Economic Extinction-Proofing

When the asteroid struck 65 million years ago, it didn't just kill dinosaurs—it killed their inability to adapt. Creatures that thrived under one set of conditions suddenly found themselves in an unrecognizable world of ash, scarcity, and upheaval. Those who could not adjust—no matter their size, speed, or ferocity—vanished. But the small, the quick, the resourceful? They found ways to survive, and their descendants live on today.

The modern economy works the same way. Every decade, sometimes every year, the rules shift. Industries collapse, new technologies rise, currencies fluctuate, and social patterns mutate. Just like the dinosaurs, you are faced with a simple ultimatum: adapt or die. But unlike the helpless giants of prehistory, you have a choice—and wealth favors the adaptable.

The Fossilized Mindset vs. The Adaptive Mindset

Most people live with a **fossilized mindset**. They cling to old methods of making money, old job structures, and old promises of security that no longer exist. They believe a single degree, a single job, or a single income stream will carry them through life. That mindset is already extinct—it just hasn't realized it yet.

The **adaptive mindset**, by contrast, thrives on change. Instead of fearing disruption, it anticipates it. Instead of clinging to outdated models, it experiments with new ones. Adaptors diversify their income, learn continuously, and see volatility as an opportunity rather than a threat. They are financial predators in a world of prey, always ready to pivot to a new food source when the old one runs dry.

Lessons from Prehistoric Survivors

The creatures that outlived the dinosaurs did so through three key traits:

1. **Flexibility in diet** – Mammals, birds, and reptiles that survived ate whatever they could find, from seeds to carrion. Economic equivalent: diversify your income and assets, don't rely on a single "food source."
2. **Rapid reproduction and experimentation** – Species that survived adapted quickly across generations. Economic equivalent: test small financial experiments, fail fast, and adjust until you find models that work.
3. **Resilience to scarcity** – Survivors could withstand long periods without abundance. Economic equivalent: build savings reserves, create fallback systems, and prepare for lean seasons so you are never desperate prey.

The Financial Asteroids of Today

Asteroids still strike—but now they take the form of:

- **Recessions and market crashes** – wiping out those who over-leverage and fail to prepare.
- **Technological disruption** – AI, automation, and new industries making entire careers obsolete overnight.
- **Inflation and debt traps** – silent predators that slowly devour the passive and unaware.
- **Global crises** – pandemics, wars, and resource shortages reshaping economies in months, not centuries.

The unprepared become financial fossils. The adaptable evolve into financial predators.

Building Your Extinction-Proof Wealth Strategy

To avoid becoming prey to the next economic asteroid, you must **engineer resilience into your financial ecosystem**. That means adopting tactics that mimic prehistoric survivors while leveraging modern wealth-building tools.

1. **Diversify Your Hunting Grounds**
    - Don't rely on a single income source. Build multiple "prey trails" through investments, side businesses, royalties, or skill monetization.
    - Treat each income stream as a different ecosystem: if one collapses, the others sustain you.
2. **Evolve Your Skills Relentlessly**
    - Survival belongs to the learner, not the static. Your skill set must mutate to match modern needs—digital literacy, financial literacy, creative adaptability.
    - Make continuous learning a survival reflex, not a luxury.
3. **Fortify Against Scarcity Seasons**
    - Just as mammals stored fat for lean winters, you must build reserves. Emergency funds, investment cushions, and strategic resource allocation give you breathing room when economies shift.
4. **Hunt Like a Predator, Not a Scavenger**
    - Predators choose their targets; scavengers wait. Wealth requires proactive opportunity-hunting: spotting undervalued assets, emerging industries, or neglected niches before the herd arrives.
5. **Develop Economic Camouflage**
    - In nature, the ability to blend into the environment meant survival. In finance, it means discretion, strategy, and avoiding unnecessary exposure to predators like taxes, debt, or predatory contracts.

The Dinosaurs of Modern Finance

Think of the companies, industries, and individuals who refused to adapt: Blockbuster, Kodak, Toys "R" Us. All once mighty, all reduced to fossils because they ignored the shifting landscape. Meanwhile, their competitors evolved. Netflix didn't just adapt; it hunted ahead of the curve. Apple didn't cling to the past—it mutated continuously. Amazon didn't play safe—it expanded into every ecosystem it could reach.

The same choice is before you. You can be a lumbering financial dinosaur or an adaptive financial predator.

The First Law of Wealth Evolution

If you do not adapt, you will be devoured.

Every financial move you make must ask this question: *Am I evolving toward resilience, or am I clinging to extinction?*

Those who adapt with speed and foresight not only survive—they dominate. By mastering adaptability, you don't just avoid being crushed by economic asteroids. You learn to ride them, using their shockwaves to propel yourself forward while others crumble.

Closing Pulse of Chapter One

Wealth is not about playing safe in a familiar field—it's about evolving as the terrain shifts beneath you. The world will never stop throwing asteroids, and safety is an illusion. What's real is your ability to adapt, pivot, and rise stronger each time.

The age of passive prey is over. The era of financial predators has begun. And your first step in this evolution is simple: refuse to fossilize.

Chapter Two – Territory and Dominance: Controlling Your Financial Hunting Grounds

In the prehistoric world, survival wasn't only about adaptability—it was also about **territory**. Dinosaurs weren't simply creatures of flesh and bone; they were rulers of landscapes. A predator without territory was a predator without food, shelter, or security. From the smallest raptor pack to the towering Tyrannosaurus Rex, dominance over land determined who ate and who starved. The lesson is clear: in both prehistory and modern life, control of territory defines power.

Your **financial hunting ground** is the arena where you seek, secure, and defend your wealth. It is the sum of your chosen industries, your career space, your digital presence, your investments, and the resources you control. Just as a predator marked its domain with scent, intimidation, or sheer presence, you must establish your financial dominance where you choose to play. Without territory, you wander aimlessly. With it, you thrive.

Why Territory Matters in Wealth

A hunter without territory starves. In today's world, territory translates into:

- **Skill Dominance**: The fields of expertise you control so thoroughly that others cannot displace you easily.
- **Market Presence**: The niche, audience, or customer base where your influence is so strong competitors hesitate to challenge you.
- **Asset Control**: The land, businesses, intellectual property, or investments that generate recurring resources within your domain.
- **Psychological Ownership**: The inner certainty that "this space belongs to me"—whether that space is your career, a financial niche, or an investment sector.

Where you establish territory, you create leverage. Where you fail to claim territory, you remain vulnerable.

Prehistoric Laws of Territory and Their Wealth Equivalents

1. **Claim Before Others Do**
    - Dinosaurs defended territories by arriving early and asserting dominance.
    - Financial equivalent: identify underdeveloped markets, industries, or niches and establish presence before they become crowded. Early movers secure the richest resources.
2. **Mark and Defend the Boundaries**
    - Territory without defense invites challengers.
    - Financial equivalent: protect your income streams with legal structures, branding, intellectual property rights, and contracts that make your claim undeniable.
3. **Expand Strategically**
    - Apex predators didn't just hold land; they pushed into new ground as resources demanded.
    - Financial equivalent: once your first income territory is secured, expand into complementary ones—investments, businesses, or digital platforms. But expand only where resources and energy allow.
4. **Respect Ecosystem Balance**
    - Overhunting a territory led to collapse. Survivors maintained balance by leaving breeding grounds intact.
    - Financial equivalent: don't extract so aggressively that your income sources dry up. Reinvest profits, nurture customer trust, and ensure longevity in your financial ecosystem.

The Myth of Shared Hunting Grounds

In the wild, predators rarely share territory unless resources are overwhelmingly abundant. The same is true financially. Too many people fall into the trap of competing in overcrowded markets where profit margins vanish. They enter industries already saturated with scavengers, leaving themselves to fight over scraps.

The predator mindset asks: *Where is the territory no one else is hunting yet?* This may be an emerging industry, a neglected demographic, or a specialized skill no one has mastered. Wealth lies in territory with low competition but high potential prey.

Building Your Financial Territory

To control your hunting ground, you must:

1. **Choose Your Domain Intentionally**
    - Don't scatter your energy across fields where you cannot dominate. Pick one or two industries, niches, or financial strategies where your skills and instincts give you the upper hand.
    - Ask yourself: *What territory can I own, not just visit?*
2. **Create an Ecosystem Within It**
    - A territory is not just a plot of land—it's an ecosystem of prey, resources, and allies. Financially, this means building multiple revenue streams within the same territory. For example: an author doesn't only sell books—they sell courses, merchandise, and licensing. A real estate investor doesn't just flip properties—they rent, syndicate, and finance.
3. **Defend with Reputation and Strategy**
    - Dinosaurs defended with teeth and claws; you defend with credibility, contracts, and strategy. Build a reputation that warns competitors: *This ground is already taken.*

4. **Establish Scarcity and Exclusivity**
    - Territory becomes valuable when others can't access it. In finance, this means making yourself hard to replace. Own intellectual property, rare skills, or unique offers that no one else can duplicate.

The Psychology of Dominance

Dominance isn't only external—it's psychological. The predator carries an aura that deters challengers. You must project financial dominance by the way you present yourself, the clarity of your decisions, and the confidence in your strategy.

- **Timidity invites predators.** If you hesitate, someone hungrier will seize your opportunity.
- **Confidence deters challengers.** When you move decisively, others second-guess whether they should risk confrontation.
- **Consistency builds dominance.** A predator that consistently patrols its territory becomes synonymous with it. In finance, consistency in output, branding, and strategy cements your control.

Territory and the Modern Predator's Toolkit

In prehistoric times, claws and teeth defined dominance. In the modern age, your toolkit includes:

- **Contracts** – your legal fangs.
- **Branding and identity** – your roar that marks the land.
- **Networking and alliances** – your pack, ensuring you are never alone against competition.
- **Capital and cash flow** – your energy reserves, fueling both defense and expansion.

Case Studies: Prehistoric Finance in Action

- **Amazon** – Began with books, claimed digital retail as territory, and expanded into streaming, cloud computing, and beyond.
- **Tesla** – Entered electric vehicles early, established dominance, then expanded into batteries and energy.
- **Small entrepreneurs** – From YouTubers to real estate investors, the story is the same: claim territory, dominate it, then grow.

Each of these examples reflects the law of territory. They didn't fight in overcrowded hunting grounds—they created their own.

Closing Pulse of Chapter Two

Wealth is not random luck. It is the result of securing, defending, and expanding your financial hunting grounds with the precision of a predator. Without territory, you are at the mercy of others. With it, you feed yourself, your family, and your future.

You are no longer wandering prey. You are a predator who marks and rules territory. The next step? Learning to dominate not just land, but **time and opportunity**—because in the prehistoric jungle of wealth, those who control timing control survival.

Chapter Three – Predatory Investing: Strike-First Mindsets and Wealth Timing

In the ancient jungles and swamps of prehistory, timing was everything. The predator that struck too early risked exhausting itself before the kill. The predator that struck too late found its prey gone—or worse, discovered that another, stronger hunter had already claimed the prize. The most successful dinosaurs, from cunning raptors to massive apex beasts, mastered the art of waiting, watching, and lunging at precisely the right moment.

Modern wealth follows the same law: those who understand **when to move, when to wait, and when to strike first** control the flow of resources. Investing is not passive—it's predatory. To thrive financially, you must think not as a timid scavenger hoping for leftovers but as a predator who stalks opportunity, positions silently, and then pounces with decisive force.

The Predator's Law of Timing

Predators don't strike randomly; their instincts refine three critical phases:

1. **Observation** – Scanning the terrain, noting patterns, sensing weaknesses in prey or openings in the environment.
   Wealth equivalent: Researching markets, industries, and opportunities before capital is deployed.
2. **Positioning** – Moving silently into place, close enough to strike without being seen.
   Wealth equivalent: Accumulating knowledge, building capital reserves, networking, and preparing to enter before the herd notices.
3. **Execution** – The decisive strike: fast, brutal, and final.
   Wealth equivalent: Making the investment, buying into undervalued assets, launching at the perfect market inflection point.

The predator who follows these phases thrives. The one who rushes in without patience, or hesitates past the moment of opportunity, starves.

Strike-First Mindsets in Wealth

The wealthiest predators of modern times have one thing in common: they **strike before others recognize opportunity**.

- **Venture capitalists** who see disruptive startups before Wall Street acknowledges them.
- **Real estate pioneers** who purchase land before development arrives.
- **Investors** who buy into commodities, digital currencies, or technologies before mainstream adoption.

This isn't luck—it's predatory awareness. They train themselves to sense shifts in the ecosystem and move before the herd.

Herd Mentality vs. Predator Instinct

The herd waits for safety. It waits for confirmation. It waits until "everyone else is doing it." But by the time the herd moves, the lush hunting grounds have already been stripped bare.

The predator thrives on **asymmetry**:

- Buy when fear dominates, sell when greed blinds the herd.
- Accumulate when assets are undervalued, distribute when others clamor to overpay.
- Strike during downturns when others are paralyzed.

In short: **the predator invests where others hesitate.**

Prehistoric Parallels for Modern Investing

- **The Ambush Raptor** – Raptors worked in packs, striking swiftly from ambush. *Wealth lesson*: collaborate with allies, syndicates, or partnerships to time group investments that amplify your power.
- **The Crocodilian Survivors** – Crocodiles have survived virtually unchanged for millions of years by waiting for the exact moment to strike. *Wealth lesson*: patience is as powerful as action. Don't force trades or investments; let the opportunity approach.
- **The Apex Hunter** – The T-Rex didn't chase every small prey—it conserved energy for big kills. *Wealth lesson*: focus your resources on high-impact investments instead of scattering them on scraps.

Wealth Timing: Reading the Ecosystem

Timing isn't just about instinct—it's about reading signals:

1. **Economic Seasons**
    - Just as ecosystems cycle through drought and abundance, economies cycle through booms and recessions. The predator watches for these seasons, preparing to strike hardest during scarcity when competition weakens.
2. **Market Signals**
    - Track indicators like interest rates, technological adoption curves, and consumer sentiment. These are footprints in the mud—signs of where prey is moving.
3. **Emerging Niches**
    - Entire species of opportunity evolve in silence before bursting into dominance. Crypto, AI, clean energy—all began as small prey herds unnoticed by apex predators. By the time the herd arrives, the feast is over.

Strike-First Wealth Tactics

To adopt a predator's strike-first investing mindset, you must practice the following:

1. **Build a War Chest**
    - Predators strike only when they have the energy. For you, this means accumulating liquid capital that allows immediate action when opportunities appear. No war chest, no strike.
2. **Train Pattern Recognition**
    - Study market behaviors until you see cycles repeating. Like a hunter tracking prey, you must know when the herd is restless, when it will migrate, and when it will fall into your trap.
3. **Exploit Weakness**
    - Prey is most vulnerable when distracted, exhausted, or isolated. In finance, this means distressed assets, undervalued companies, or overlooked opportunities.
4. **Act Without Hesitation**
    - Once the moment arrives, predators don't debate. They strike. Wealth favors speed. When you've done your research, hesitation is fatal.

Avoiding the Scavenger Trap

Scavengers feed on leftovers, scraps, and corpses. In wealth, scavengers:

- Wait for mainstream news to announce opportunities.
- Buy at the top of bubbles when everyone else is euphoric.
- Settle for low returns because they fear bold moves.

Scavengers survive—but never dominate. Predators create wealth; scavengers inherit scraps.

Case Studies in Predatory Wealth Timing

- **Warren Buffett** – Known for buying during crises, striking when others flee. His mantra: "Be fearful when others are greedy, and greedy when others are fearful." Pure predator timing.
- **Elon Musk** – Entered industries (EVs, private space, solar) when they were dismissed as impossible. A strike-first mindset that redefined entire markets.
- **Amazon** – Shifted aggressively from books into cloud computing before the herd even understood the term. A predatory ambush that now dominates an entire ecosystem.

Closing Pulse of Chapter Three

Predatory investing is about **position, patience, and precision**. It is about striking first—not recklessly, but with perfect timing honed by preparation.

The herd will always be late. Scavengers will always fight over scraps. But you—the predator—learn to watch quietly, build strength, and strike with force at the moment of maximum opportunity.

Wealth doesn't reward the timid. It rewards the hunter who dares to pounce.

Chapter Four – Predator Timing: Striking When Opportunity is Ripe

In the prehistoric wild, even the fiercest predator lived or died by timing. A raptor that lunged too soon risked startling its prey into escape. A T-Rex that waited too long could lose a meal to faster hunters. Crocodiles, unchanged for millions of years, embody this law: they lie in wait, still as stone, until the perfect moment presents itself—then, in an instant, they strike with devastating force. Timing, not brute strength, determined survival.

The modern wealth ecosystem follows the same rhythm. Money doesn't flow evenly—it pulses in seasons, cycles, and waves. Those who strike when the opportunity is ripe feast on abundance, while those who hesitate, or act prematurely, starve. Mastering predator timing means learning to sense the rhythms of the financial jungle and aligning your strike with the moment of maximum impact.

The Pulse of Opportunity

Every economy, market, and industry has a heartbeat. It contracts and expands, surges and retreats. Opportunity ripens like fruit on a branch—it is green and bitter if you pluck too soon, rotten if you wait too long. The predator mindset requires three things:

1. **Patience** – Resist striking before the prey is vulnerable.
2. **Preparedness** – Position yourself so that when the moment comes, you are ready.
3. **Precision** – Strike in a way that secures maximum yield with minimal wasted effort.

In wealth, this translates to resisting hype, preparing capital and strategy in advance, and executing decisively when the window opens.

Recognizing Ripe Conditions

How does the predator know when the moment has come? By reading the environment.

1. **Economic Seasons**
    - Like droughts and floods, economies cycle through expansion and contraction. Recessions often bring ripe conditions—assets undervalued, competitors weak, fear clouding the herd's judgment. The predator strikes hardest here.
2. **Technological Shifts**
    - When a new tool, platform, or innovation emerges, it often passes through phases: dismissed, resisted, accepted, and then demanded. The ripe moment comes in the phase between resistance and acceptance—before the herd realizes its value.
3. **Market Signals**
    - Just as prey leave footprints and broken branches, financial ecosystems leave clues. Price dips, undervaluation, sudden scarcity, or surges in adoption are all signals that the fruit is ripe for harvest.
4. **Competitor Fatigue**
    - Prey is easiest to take when tired. Financially, this means entering markets where others have grown complacent, disorganized, or overleveraged.

The Dangers of Premature Strikes

Even predators fall when they mistake eagerness for readiness. In finance, premature strikes look like:

- **Buying into hype too early** before proof of value exists.
- **Over-leveraging** before systems are stable.
- **Entering markets** before infrastructure or adoption supports growth.

The result is wasted energy, capital loss, and vulnerability to real predators waiting in the shadows. Timing is the difference between fortune and fossilization.

The Fatal Cost of Hesitation

Yet hesitation can be deadlier than premature action. Prey doesn't linger forever. If you hesitate at the moment of ripeness:

- Competitors pounce first, leaving scraps.
- Prices rise sharply, pushing you into the scavenger's trap.
- The opportunity window closes, sometimes for decades.

The predator knows: hesitation costs more than mistakes. Mistakes can be corrected; missed opportunities never return.

The Art of Stalking Time

Predators don't stumble into opportunity—they stalk it. Wealth hunters must practice the same art:

1. **Preparation** – Keep capital, networks, and systems ready. The strike must be immediate, not delayed by scrambling.
2. **Pattern Recognition** – Study cycles and anticipate when opportunities typically emerge. Just as predators learn migrations, investors learn booms and busts.
3. **Controlled Stillness** – Sometimes the greatest action is waiting, resisting distraction until conditions align.
4. **Explosive Decisiveness** – When the time comes, unleash with full force. Commit, invest, launch, buy—without half measures.

Timing Case Studies in Wealth

- **The 2008 Financial Crisis** – While most fled, predators with patience and cash reserves bought real estate and stocks at historic lows. Their timing created fortunes that last to this day.
- **Apple and the iPhone** – They did not launch the first smartphone but waited until technology, consumer readiness, and ecosystem infrastructure aligned. Their timing defined a generation.
- **Bitcoin and Crypto** – Early adopters who struck during resistance, before mass acceptance, turned small bets into empires. Latecomers, acting after ripeness had passed, often lost.

Developing Predator Timing Instincts

1. **Build War Readiness** – Without capital reserves, patience is meaningless. Keep liquid resources ready for strikes.
2. **Study Ecosystems Daily** – Observe markets, industries, and consumer behaviors until patterns become second nature.
3. **Learn Contrarian Patience** – Train yourself to act when others hesitate and to hold still when others stampede.
4. **Sharpen Decisive Reflexes** – Set personal rules: if X condition is met, strike. Eliminate hesitation with pre-built strategies.

The Rhythm of Wealth Evolution

Timing is not a one-time skill but an ongoing rhythm. Like the tides of prehistoric swamps, opportunities rise and fall. Master predators didn't eat once—they fed continually, striking at one ripe moment after another. Wealth hunters do the same: building momentum, layering victories, and sustaining dominance over decades.

Closing Pulse of Chapter Four

Predator timing is the art of aligning instinct, preparation, and decisive execution with the ripeness of opportunity. It is about knowing that the world does not reward the earliest or the loudest—it rewards the one who strikes at the *exact moment of advantage*.

The scavenger acts too late. The reckless predator acts too soon. The wealth predator acts **on time**—and on time is always just before the herd even realizes the fruit is ready.

When you master timing, you no longer chase opportunity. You anticipate it, stalk it, and devour it the moment it ripens.

Chapter Five – The Pack Advantage: Building Alliances for Shared Hunts

In the prehistoric wild, not every predator ruled alone. While the T-Rex embodied solitary dominance, raptors thrived by banding together. Their strength wasn't in size but in **coordination, communication, and shared purpose**. One raptor could not take down prey many times its size—but a pack could. This is the essence of the pack advantage: when individuals unite, they amplify one another's strengths, cover weaknesses, and secure rewards that would have been impossible alone.

The same law applies to wealth. The lone wolf entrepreneur can achieve much, but the predator who forms alliances—whether through partnerships, networks, or syndicates—multiplies their reach and resilience. The modern financial ecosystem is too vast, too volatile, and too competitive to hunt alone forever. To build enduring wealth, you must learn to identify, attract, and lead—or join—packs that hunt together.

The Law of the Pack

Nature teaches that the pack thrives when:

1. **Roles are Defined** – Some chase, some ambush, some finish the kill.
   Wealth equivalent: partners bring complementary skills—vision, execution, finance, marketing, strategy.
2. **Communication is Clear** – Confusion in the hunt means prey escapes.
   Wealth equivalent: transparency in goals, agreements, and expectations prevents collapse.
3. **The Spoils are Shared** – Packs collapse when selfishness dominates.
   Wealth equivalent: clear profit-sharing, equity arrangements, and mutual benefit cement alliances.
4. **Trust is Non-Negotiable** – Packs only succeed if every member knows the others will strike together.
   Wealth equivalent: alliances must be based on credibility, integrity, and a proven track record.

Why Go It Alone Is Extinction Thinking

Many wealth-builders cling to the illusion of solitary power: *"I don't need anyone. I'll do it all myself."* But this is fossilized thinking. Consider:

- No empire was ever built by one person. Every king had generals, advisors, armies.
- No modern corporation functions without teams, shareholders, and networks.
- Even investors leverage syndicates, angel groups, and joint ventures.

The solitary predator may score occasional victories, but the pack predator creates empires.

Building Wealth Packs in the Modern World

1. **Partnerships and Joint Ventures**
    - Just as raptors combined speed with strategy, entrepreneurs and investors form alliances to combine resources, networks, and skill sets. Example: a creative visionary partnering with a financial strategist.
2. **Networks and Communities**
    - Packs aren't always tight-knit teams; sometimes they're looser networks of allies. Mastermind groups, professional associations, and digital communities allow predators to share intelligence and opportunities.
3. **Syndicates and Investment Packs**
    - In prehistoric terms, this is a coordinated ambush. In modern terms, it's pooling capital for real estate deals, venture investments, or business acquisitions. What one predator could not purchase, the pack secures easily.
4. **Mentorship and Hierarchy**
    - Packs often have alpha leaders and experienced hunters teaching the young. In wealth, mentors accelerate your learning curve and help you avoid costly mistakes, while you pass value downward to your pack.

The Pack Predator's Advantage

When you hunt with a pack, you gain:

- **Leverage** – One predator cannot chase multiple prey, but a pack can. Shared efforts multiply results.
- **Resilience** – If one predator falls sick, the pack sustains itself. Alliances protect against individual weakness.
- **Intelligence** – Multiple eyes and instincts scan the ecosystem, spotting opportunities faster than a lone hunter.
- **Dominance** – A lone wolf may be challenged, but a pack projects power that deters rivals.

The Dangers of a Weak Pack

Not all packs thrive. Some implode from within. Beware of alliances that:

- **Lack Clear Leadership** – Without direction, hunts dissolve into chaos.
- **Contain Hidden Predators** – Not all allies hunt for the pack; some hunt for themselves, sabotaging trust.
- **Are Built on Scarcity Thinking** – If allies focus only on short-term scraps, they will abandon long-term strategy.

To build strong packs, you must be selective. Not every predator deserves your trust.

Prehistoric Strategy for Modern Application

- **Raptor Tactics** – Work in small, highly coordinated groups that specialize in agility and precision. Wealth equivalent: agile startup teams or boutique investment groups.
- **Wolf Dynamics** – Establish loyalty, hierarchy, and shared survival. Wealth equivalent: long-term business partnerships where members trust each other deeply.
- **Lion Prides** – Blend protection, nurturing, and collective hunting. Wealth equivalent: family businesses or legacy wealth-building alliances across generations.

Wealth Packs in Action: Case Studies

- **Silicon Valley Founders** – Many of the most successful companies were not solo ventures but built by founding teams who complemented each other's strengths (e.g., Jobs and Wozniak at Apple, Page and Brin at Google).
- **Investment Syndicates** – Groups of angel investors pool funds to secure stakes in startups that individuals could not access alone.
- **Mastermind Alliances** – Entrepreneurs like Napoleon Hill's "Think and Grow Rich" examples used collective brainstorming packs to leap forward faster than isolation ever allowed.

Building Your Own Pack

1. **Identify Your Strengths and Weaknesses**
    - Know what role you play in the hunt—visionary, strategist, builder, financier. Find allies who balance your weaknesses.
2. **Select with Ruthless Precision**
    - Not everyone deserves a seat in your pack. Choose allies based on trust, competence, and proven loyalty.
3. **Establish Rules of the Hunt**
    - Contracts, agreements, and clear expectations prevent conflict. The pack must know how spoils are shared.
4. **Commit to the Long Game**
    - A pack that fractures after one hunt isn't a pack—it's a coincidence. Build alliances with durability and shared purpose beyond a single deal.

Closing Pulse of Chapter Five

The lone predator can survive—but the pack predator can dominate. In finance, alliances expand your reach, amplify your strength, and ensure survival when the ecosystem shifts. The wealthiest predators of history—from empires to corporations—were never solitary.

The question is no longer *if* you need a pack, but *which pack you will build or join.* For in the modern jungle of wealth, the solitary predator is an endangered species, while the pack hunters feast on opportunities too vast for any one creature to claim.

Chapter Six – Herd Strategies vs. Solo Hunting: Which Wealth Path Fits Your DNA?

In the age of dinosaurs, not every creature lived by the tooth and claw of solitary hunting. Some found safety and sustenance in numbers. Herds of hadrosaurs, triceratops, and sauropods moved together, overwhelming predators with sheer scale and shared vigilance. Others—like raptors, tyrannosaurs, and early mammals—thrived through independent or small-group hunting, relying on stealth, timing, and personal cunning. Both strategies worked—but only for the species designed for them.

Wealth works the same way. Some thrive in the collective—leveraging teams, institutions, or communities to secure stability and growth. Others thrive as lone predators—staking personal territory, making independent plays, and embracing risk in ways herds never could. To know which wealth path fits you, you must examine your instincts, your environment, and your long-term vision.

The Herd Strategy: Safety in Numbers

Herds survive not by superiority, but by **collective protection**. When predators strike, individuals may fall, but the group endures. Translated to modern wealth:

1. **Stability Over Risk**
   - Herd-minded individuals prefer structured paths: salaried careers, corporate ladders, pensions, and group investment vehicles like index funds.
   - They value predictability, even if the returns are modest.
2. **Shared Vigilance**
   - In herds, many eyes scan the horizon for danger. In finance, this is diversification spread across institutions, groupthink protection, and reliance on advisors or systems.
3. **Strength in Size**
   - Herd strategies excel when large movements matter—such as unionized industries, government-backed retirement accounts, or collective negotiations.
4. **Sacrifice of Autonomy**
   - To gain safety, herd creatures surrender independence. In wealth, this means your growth is tethered to the group's pace, not your own.

Pros: Stability, lower risk, safety nets, built-in protection against total collapse.

Cons: Limited growth, slower wealth accumulation, vulnerability to systemic shifts (if the herd stampedes off a cliff, everyone falls together).

The Solo Predator Strategy: Independence and Risk

Solo hunters live and die by their own instincts. Their success is not guaranteed by numbers but by **personal timing, power, and cunning**. In wealth terms, the solo predator chooses independence over safety.

1. **Direct Control**
    - Solo wealth builders choose their own prey—investments, businesses, or ventures. They thrive when they dictate their pace rather than following the herd.
2. **High Risk, High Reward**
    - Like a lone raptor, they may starve if they miss a kill—but when successful, they claim the full reward without sharing.
3. **Agility and Flexibility**
    - Herds move slowly; predators pivot instantly. Entrepreneurs, traders, and innovators excel here, moving ahead of the masses into new opportunities.
4. **Isolation Danger**
    - Without a pack or herd, failure rests solely on the individual. Resilience and resourcefulness must replace collective safety.

Pros: Unlimited upside, independence, ability to pivot quickly, potential to dominate unique niches.

Cons: High vulnerability to mistakes, greater emotional strain, and lack of built-in support.

Hybrid Paths: Packs and Semi-Herds
Between herd and solo lie hybrid models:

- **The Pack Predator (Chapter Five)** – Small alliances where risk and reward are shared strategically, combining agility with support.
- **The Cooperative Herd-Predator Blend** – Individuals who join collectives (like mastermind groups or syndicates) but still make bold independent moves.
- **The Lone Wolf Among Herds** – An individual who uses the herd for camouflage (a corporate career or stable investments) while quietly building personal wealth plays on the side.

These hybrids offer the flexibility of the predator with the stability of the herd.

Prehistoric Case Studies in Wealth Behavior

1. **The Sauropod Herds** – Massive herds of long-necked giants overwhelmed predators by sheer presence. Wealth equivalent: pension funds, mutual funds, and government-backed security systems. Reliable, but slow.
2. **The Triceratops Circle** – Herd members defended each other when threatened. Wealth equivalent: unions, co-ops, and family-owned wealth pools.
3. **The Tyrannosaurus** – Dominant solo predator. Wealth equivalent: entrepreneurs who seize industries through personal dominance (think Rockefeller, Musk).
4. **The Velociraptor Pack** – Blending hunting intelligence and alliances. Wealth equivalent: startups, joint ventures, and syndicates.

How to Know Your DNA

Not every wealth strategy fits every predator—or herbivore. To choose your path, ask:

1. **Do I value stability or freedom more?**
    - Stability leans herd; freedom leans predator.
2. **How do I handle risk and failure?**
    - Fear of loss suggests herd safety. Thrill of risk suggests predator hunting.
3. **Do I thrive alone or in groups?**
    - Comfort in teams suggests herd or pack dynamics. Independence suggests predator.
4. **What's my long-term wealth vision?**
    - If you want consistent, predictable growth, herd strategies serve you. If you want empire-building and dominance, predator paths call louder.

Modern Wealth Lessons from the Herd vs. Predator Divide

- **Herd Wealth Builders** rely on: careers, retirement accounts, real estate for stability, group investments.
- **Predator Wealth Builders** rely on: startups, trading, aggressive investments, intellectual property, disruptive innovation.
- **Hybrid Hunters** mix both: a stable herd path for security while making calculated predator strikes for acceleration.

Neither is "wrong"—but mismatch is fatal. A predator forced into a herd suffocates. A herd creature thrown into predator play is eaten alive.

Closing Pulse of Chapter Six

In the prehistoric wild, both herds and predators thrived—but only by staying true to their nature. Wealth operates by the same law. The question isn't which is better, but **which is right for you**.

Are you the stable grazer, safe in numbers?
Are you the lone predator, carving territory by tooth and claw?
Or are you the hybrid hunter, straddling both worlds to balance safety with dominance?

To survive—and to thrive—you must know your financial DNA. Choose wrong, and extinction looms. Choose right, and your wealth evolution accelerates beyond imagination.

Chapter Seven – Resource Hoarding and Seasonal Wealth: Thriving in Scarcity and Abundance

In the prehistoric wild, survival was never constant. The world shifted with cycles of **abundance and scarcity**. Rainforests flourished, then burned. Rivers swelled, then dried. Herds of prey animals grew large in fertile seasons, then dwindled when food vanished. Those who survived were not the strongest or even the fiercest—they were the creatures who **prepared for cycles**, hoarding when times were plentiful and conserving when famine arrived.

The same law applies to wealth. Economies boom and bust. Markets soar, then crash. Entire industries flourish, then vanish. Those who treat abundance as permanent are always shocked by scarcity. Those who anticipate both seasons—and build strategies for each—are the ones who not only survive, but dominate.

The Cyclical Law of Wealth

1. **Abundance Is Temporary**
   Prey herds grew massive in lush seasons, but eventually predators overhunted them or the vegetation collapsed. In wealth, bull markets and economic booms never last forever. Assuming they will is financial suicide.
2. **Scarcity Is Inevitable**
   Droughts, volcanic winters, and famine came for every ecosystem. Likewise, recessions, inflation, and crises will always return. Scarcity is not an exception—it is a recurring season.
3. **Reserves Equal Survival**
   Crocodiles lived off fat stores, mammals cached food in dens, and birds migrated with seeds in their bellies. Financial survivors mirror this behavior with savings, diversified investments, and fallback plans.

4.Opportunity Shifts in Scarcity

During famine, predators thrived by hunting weakened prey. In finance, downturns present the best opportunities: cheap assets, collapsing competitors, and undervalued markets.

Resource Hoarding: Preparing for the Famine

Resource hoarding was not greed—it was foresight. In wealth terms, this means:

- **Emergency Reserves**: Maintain 6–12 months of liquid capital to ensure survival in downturns. This "fat storage" buys freedom when others panic.
- **Diversified Resource Storage**: Don't rely on a single source of income or one type of asset. Spread your reserves across cash, property, equities, commodities, royalties, and intellectual property.
- **Hidden Stashes**: Just as prehistoric creatures concealed caches from rivals, store some reserves in protected or discreet forms (trusts, secondary accounts, or assets outside the public eye).
- **Abundance Allocation**: In plentiful seasons, consciously set aside wealth. Predators that gorge without storing collapse in famine.

Thriving in Seasonal Shifts

In Times of Abundance (Boom Cycles, Bull Markets):

- **Expand Territory**: Grow your business, pursue high-return investments, and scale ventures.
- **Stockpile**: Allocate profits into reserves rather than overspending or over-leveraging.
- **Resist Illusions of Permanence**: Avoid assuming the good times will last forever. Build safety nets even as you feast.

In Times of Scarcity (Recessions, Crashes, Crises):

- **Defend Core Resources**: Protect essential income streams and trim unnecessary expenditures.
- **Strike Opportunistically**: Just as weakened prey are easiest to take, acquire undervalued assets or businesses while rivals retreat.
- **Ration Your Reserves**: Use savings strategically, not recklessly. Each deployment of capital should serve a long-term gain.

Psychological Traps of the Seasons

- **Abundance Trap**: Greed, recklessness, and overextension. When everyone feels invincible, discipline becomes rare—and predators who resist the trap build lasting empires.
- **Scarcity Trap**: Fear, paralysis, and missed opportunities. In downturns, most freeze or flee. True predators see these moments as their richest hunting grounds.

Ancient Survival, Modern Wealth

- **Migration = Industry Shift**: When the land went barren, herds migrated. In wealth, you must pivot industries or markets when old ones die.
- **Caching = Diversified Investments**: Prehistoric mammals buried food in many places. You should bury wealth in many vehicles—stocks, real estate, IP, and commodities.
- **Fat Storage = Cash Reserves**: Crocodiles lived months without food. You must live months without income when downturns hit.
- **Predation in Scarcity = Counter-Cyclical Investing**: Predators thrived when prey weakened. In finance, buy assets when others are desperate to sell.

Case Studies of Seasonal Wealth

- **Great Depression Fortunes**: Families with cash reserves bought land, businesses, and real estate at historic lows, creating dynasties that still thrive.
- **Post-Crisis Expansion**: Investors who stockpiled before 2008 acquired properties and stocks at a discount, multiplying wealth while others collapsed.
- **Corporate Survivors**: Companies like Amazon and Apple weathered downturns by hoarding cash in abundance, then expanding aggressively during recessions.

Building Your Seasonal Wealth Blueprint

1. **Hoard in Discipline**: Decide what percentage of every windfall or profit season will go into reserves. Treat hoarding as non-negotiable.
2. **Track the Seasons**: Watch market cycles, consumer behavior, and global patterns. Know whether abundance or scarcity is rising.
3. **Design Scarcity Maneuvers**: Have a lean-budget and survival plan prepared before crises hit.
4. **Train Counter-Cyclical Instincts**: Rewire yourself to see downturns not as threats, but as ambush opportunities for wealth predators.

Closing Pulse of Chapter Seven

Survival was never about size, speed, or even dominance. It was about seasonal intelligence. Prehistoric creatures thrived by **anticipating cycles**—feasting and storing in abundance, conserving and striking in scarcity. Wealth follows the exact same law.

The herd feasts until collapse. The scavenger waits for scraps. But the predator who hoards wisely and hunts with timing uses both abundance and scarcity as allies.

This is the foundation of financial immortality: to never starve in famine, to never squander in feast, and to always emerge stronger after every season passes.

Chapter Eight – Digging for Gold (and Fossils): Unearthing Rare, Long-Term Assets

Dinosaurs may have ruled the land, but their remains—bones, teeth, and fossilized treasures—outlasted them all. While most creatures vanished without a trace, the ones preserved in stone became eternal markers of their dominance. The same principle applies to wealth: the fleeting gains of day-to-day hunting can feed you for a season, but the **rare, enduring assets you unearth and protect become your fossils of fortune**—treasures that endure beyond a single lifetime.

Gold, land, intellectual property, and other long-term stores of value are today's equivalents of fossils buried beneath layers of earth. They are not obvious, nor are they immediately accessible. They require excavation, patience, and the vision to recognize that what lies beneath the surface may be worth far more than what's immediately visible. To thrive as a wealth predator, you must learn the art of digging—not just for quick prey, but for the rare assets that endure across generations.

The Nature of Rare Assets

Rare, long-term assets have three characteristics that separate them from ordinary resources:

1. **Scarcity** – Like fossils or gold veins, they exist in limited supply. The more scarce the asset, the more it resists inflation, devaluation, and time.
2. **Durability** – They last across seasons, cycles, and crises. When short-term prey disappears, rare assets remain.
3. **Legacy Value** – These are assets that can be passed down, compounding wealth across generations. Fossils became treasures not for their immediate use, but for what they represented millions of years later.

Modern Fossils: Types of Long-Term Assets

1. **Precious Metals**
    - Gold and silver have been stores of wealth for millennia. They resist inflation, remain globally recognized, and often rise in value during crises.
    - Just as fossils are unearthed with patience, gold must be slowly accumulated—not chased during hype cycles.
2. **Real Estate (The Land Beneath Your Feet)**
    - Land was the original territory of predators, and it remains the foundation of long-term wealth. Unlike businesses that rise and fall, land is finite. Real estate not only preserves value but generates cash flow.
3. **Intellectual Property (Your Mind's Fossils)**
    - Books, patents, copyrights, and trademarks are modern "fossils" of thought. They outlive their creators, continuing to generate royalties and licensing income.
    - A single intellectual fossil, properly unearthed and protected, can yield wealth for generations.
4. **Businesses With Moats**
    - Companies that dominate their niches are like rare fossil discoveries—difficult to replicate, enduring across economic cycles. Acquiring or building such businesses creates an asset that holds long-term value.
5. **Cultural Collectibles and Rarities**
    - Fossils themselves became rare commodities. In modern times, art, antiques, rare wines, and even digital assets (NFTs) can serve as enduring stores of value—if chosen wisely.

The Predator's Role as Excavator

Finding these rare assets is not like chasing prey across the open plains—it's an excavation. The predator must learn patience, research, and deep vision.

- **Surface Grazing vs. Deep Digging**
    - The herd grazes on what's visible. The predator digs where others ignore. The true treasures are rarely on the surface.
- **Tools of Excavation**
    - Knowledge, networks, and patience are your pickaxes and shovels. To unearth rare opportunities, you must look beyond mainstream plays into hidden or undervalued markets.
- **Recognizing Fossils in the Making**
    - Many assets appear ordinary until time proves their rarity. Spotting intellectual property, emerging land value, or overlooked collectibles early is the hallmark of the financial excavator.

Cyclical Patience: The Fossil Timeline

Unlike quick kills, fossils require **time to reveal their value**. The predator mindset must embrace cycles:

- **Acquisition Phase** – Digging and uncovering assets while they are undervalued or ignored.
- **Holding Phase** – Patience as the asset matures or the market awakens to its value.
- **Legacy Phase** – Passing the asset to heirs, trusts, or foundations so it continues to produce beyond your lifespan.

The herd wants instant consumption. The predator who digs for fossils thinks in decades, even centuries.

Wealth Lessons from Fossils and Gold

1. **Endurance Outweighs Flash**
    - Dinosaurs vanished, but their fossils endured. Businesses, currencies, and fads collapse, but rare assets persist.
2. **Hidden Treasures Require Work**
    - Fossils aren't found on the surface; they require excavation. Wealth predators must work harder than the herd, researching niches and overlooked markets.
3. **Patience Converts Dust Into Diamonds**
    - Fossils form over millions of years; gold requires refinement. Wealth predators must embrace patience, allowing assets to mature.

Practical Excavation Tactics

1. **Study Scarcity**
    - Ask: Is this asset finite? Will demand grow as supply diminishes? If yes, it has fossil potential.
2. **Accumulate Quietly**
    - The predator doesn't roar while digging; it gathers discreetly, avoiding herd stampedes into hype.
3. **Preserve and Protect**
    - Just as fossils need careful handling, long-term assets must be safeguarded with legal protections, trusts, or proper storage.
4. **Think in Centuries**
    - What will this be worth in 50 years? 100 years? The fossil investor plays for legacy, not just survival.

Case Studies in Fossil Wealth

- **The Rothschild Dynasty** – Amassed land, gold, and banking assets across generations, creating an enduring fossilized empire.
- **Walt Disney** – Intellectual property as fossil. His creations still generate billions decades after his death.
- **Rockefeller** – Oil, land, and monopolistic businesses became fossils of industrial wealth that endure to this day.
- **Modern Investors** – Those who bought Bitcoin when it was dismissed as a fad unearthed digital fossils now recognized as rare assets.

Closing Pulse of Chapter Eight

The quick kill may feed you today, but the fossil feeds you forever. The predator who learns to dig, to unearth, and to hold rare assets transcends the endless chase for prey. While others graze and scavenge, you excavate treasures that endure across time.

Fossils are not just relics of the past—they are metaphors for the future of wealth. Unearth them, preserve them, and let them become your dynasty's bedrock. For in the end, the true apex predator is not the one who feeds today, but the one whose wealth outlives extinction itself.

Chapter Nine – Apex Predator Positioning: Becoming the Wealth Species That Others Cannot Ignore

In the prehistoric world, not all predators were equal. Some hunted opportunistically, feeding when they could. Others were small and agile, surviving in the shadows of giants. But towering above them all stood the **apex predators**—creatures like Tyrannosaurus Rex, Giganotosaurus, and Spinosaurus. These were not just hunters; they were the undisputed rulers of their ecosystems. When they walked, everything else adjusted. Herbivores migrated. Smaller predators scavenged leftovers. Entire landscapes bent to their dominance.

In wealth, the same principle applies. There are opportunists, side hustlers, and scavengers fighting for scraps—but above them all stand the **apex wealth predators**. These individuals and enterprises position themselves so powerfully that they become impossible to ignore. Their presence reshapes industries. Their decisions ripple across markets. They do not chase opportunities—they create ecosystems where opportunities chase them.

What Does Apex Predator Positioning Mean in Wealth?

Apex predator positioning is the art of elevating your financial presence to a level where:

1. **You Control Territory** – Your industry, niche, or platform becomes synonymous with your name or brand.
2. **You Shape Ecosystems** – Competitors adapt to your moves, customers flock to your standards, and your innovations redefine markets.
3. **You Command Respect and Fear** – Rivals think twice before competing directly. Partners seek alliance rather than confrontation.
4. **You Achieve Visibility Without Pursuit** – Just as prey instinctively knew where the T-Rex hunted, wealth flows toward apex predators by reputation, not constant chasing.

The Evolutionary Ladder: From Prey to Apex

Not everyone begins at the top. To position yourself as an apex predator, you climb through evolutionary stages:

1. **Prey Stage** – Vulnerable, dependent on systems (jobs, fixed incomes, herd security).
2. **Scavenger Stage** – Living off scraps: side hustles, small plays, waiting for others to drop opportunities.
3. **Hunter Stage** – Actively chasing wealth through entrepreneurship, investing, or innovation.
4. **Pack Predator Stage** – Coordinating with others for bigger kills, leveraging partnerships and syndicates.
5. **Apex Predator Stage** – Creating and controlling ecosystems. Wealth flows toward you naturally because of your dominance and positioning.

The goal is not merely to hunt, but to **ascend the food chain until no one can ignore you.**

Traits of the Apex Wealth Predator

1. **Brand Authority**
    - Just as the roar of a T-Rex echoed across valleys, apex wealth predators establish brands so strong they command recognition.
    - This authority creates gravitational pull: customers, clients, and capital seek them instinctively.
2. **Ecosystem Control**
    - Apex predators don't just feed in ecosystems—they control them. In wealth, this means owning platforms, supply chains, or intellectual property that others rely on.
3. **Visibility as Power**
    - The apex predator doesn't need to hide. Its very visibility deters rivals. In finance, this means strategic media presence, thought leadership, and industry influence.
4. **Decisive Strikes with Scale**
    - Apex predators don't waste energy on small prey. They strike at opportunities that feed them massively. For wealth predators, this means big deals, industry-shaping investments, or empire-scale ventures.
5. **Legacy Beyond the Hunt**
    - Apex predators leave fossilized footprints across history. Wealth predators position themselves so their impact endures—dynasties, institutions, and legacies that persist beyond their lifetime.

Positioning Strategies: Becoming Impossible to Ignore

1. **Niche Domination**
    - Pick one industry or niche and make it yours. Depth builds dominance faster than shallow breadth. Amazon began with books before expanding into everything.
2. **Build a Fortress Brand**
    - Your brand is your roar. Craft it to symbolize strength, trust, and inevitability. Competitors may compete on price or features—but your brand identity remains unshakable.
3. **Control Key Resources**
    - Apex predators hold territories that others must pass through. In wealth, this means owning distribution, data, or assets critical to competitors.
4. **Create Dependency**
    - Make others reliant on your ecosystem. Apple created dependency through devices, services, and ecosystems that lock in users. Once prey enter, they rarely leave.
5. **Strategic Alliances**
    - Apex predators may hunt alone, but they often coexist with packs. Wealth predators build alliances with governments, institutions, or networks that solidify dominance.
6. **Visibility Infrastructure**
    - Be seen. Apex predators are felt in the ecosystem; their absence creates imbalance. Use media, publications, and platforms to ensure your dominance is recognized universally.

Prehistoric Parallels in Business and Wealth

- **T-Rex Economics**: The apex predator of its time, T-Rex owned the top of the food chain. Business equivalent: companies like Google and Amazon, which dominate ecosystems so thoroughly competitors merely adapt to their existence.
- **Spinosaurus Adaptability**: Thrived in both water and land environments. Wealth lesson: diversify dominance across ecosystems (multiple industries or geographic markets).
- **Raptor Coordination**: While not apex in size, raptors positioned themselves as apex through cooperation. Wealth equivalent: joint ventures that dominate niches too small for giants to notice, but too strong for rivals to enter.

Apex Predator Mistakes That Lead to Extinction

Even apex predators fell when they miscalculated. Avoid these traps:

1. **Overexpansion Without Balance** – Dinosaurs grew massive, but when resources shifted, their size became their weakness. Businesses that scale too quickly without reserves collapse under their own weight.
2. **Complacency** – Believing dominance will last forever. Blockbuster thought it owned the ecosystem—until Netflix adapted faster.
3. **Ignoring Evolution** – Apex predators that fail to adapt to climate change or new competitors eventually fall. In wealth, this means ignoring technology, market shifts, or cultural changes.

Practical Blueprint for Apex Predator Positioning

1. **Claim Your Territory**: Pick your niche and own it fully.
2. **Control Ecosystem Pathways**: Become the gatekeeper that others must work through.
3. **Roar Loudly and Strategically**: Build brand visibility across platforms.
4. **Leverage Scarcity**: Focus on rare offerings—assets, skills, or services others cannot duplicate.
5. **Protect with Moats**: Legal protections, patents, contracts, or network effects that make your dominance untouchable.
6. **Build Legacy Infrastructure**: Trusts, dynasties, and institutional wealth-building to preserve apex status beyond your lifetime.

Closing Pulse of Chapter Nine

To become an apex predator of wealth is to transcend mere survival. It is no longer about scraping together income or chasing scraps—it is about creating an ecosystem where your presence defines the game itself.

Others may hunt. Others may scavenge. But the apex predator **is the ecosystem**. Its dominance is undeniable, its influence inescapable, and its wealth untouchable.

Your mission is to rise up the evolutionary chain—not to remain prey, not to live off scraps, but to claim the throne of your financial jungle. When you achieve apex predator positioning, you no longer wonder if opportunity will come. You know it will—because in your ecosystem, **all paths lead to you.**

Chapter Ten – Apex Empire Building: Branding, Legacy, and Multi-Generational Wealth

The Extinction-Proof Dynasty: Building Wealth That Outlives You

Dinosaurs may have vanished, but their fossils endure as silent witnesses to their dominance. Entire species ruled unchallenged for millions of years, but only those who left lasting traces in stone are remembered. In wealth, the same principle applies: it is not enough to dominate in your lifetime. True apex predators of finance build **empires**—structures of branding, legacy, and wealth—that extend far beyond their personal existence. These dynasties are extinction-proof, transcending recessions, crises, and even the death of their founder.

You've mastered adaptability, territory, timing, resource hoarding, and positioning. Now comes the highest level of the predator's evolution: not simply feeding on opportunity, but creating a **permanent empire** that defines the ecosystem for generations.

The Final Law of the Apex Predator: Legacy Beyond Life

In nature, apex predators that vanished without leaving fossils disappeared without influence. But those that fossilized shaped science, myth, and culture millions of years later. In wealth, the same law governs legacy:

1. **Your Brand Is Your Fossil** – The image, message, and identity you create outlive you, guiding how the world remembers you.
2. **Your Assets Are Your Fossil Record** – Properties, intellectual property, businesses, and investments become lasting monuments of your existence.
3. **Your Dynasty Is Your Species' Survival** – Passing wealth forward ensures your bloodline and vision remain dominant long after you are gone.

Branding: The Apex Predator's Roar

Every apex predator had a presence that defined its ecosystem. For you, that presence is **your brand**.

- **Consistency**: A predator's roar was recognizable instantly; your brand must be as distinct.
- **Symbolism**: Dinosaurs were symbols of strength, speed, or intelligence. Your brand must embody values that resonate universally—power, resilience, freedom, innovation.
- **Visibility**: Apex predators did not hide; their presence influenced behavior for miles around. Your brand must command space across platforms, industries, and audiences.

Practical Steps:

1. Craft a narrative that positions you as the inevitable leader in your niche.
2. Protect your brand legally (trademarks, copyrights) so imitators cannot weaken your roar.
3. Reinforce your brand through books, media, content, and thought leadership that immortalize your presence.

Legacy: From Predator to Ancestor

Legacy is not built by consumption—it is built by **preservation and transfer**. The true predator thinks in centuries, not seasons.

- **Financial Legacy**: Assets structured in trusts, foundations, and legal entities that prevent fragmentation across generations.
- **Cultural Legacy**: Values, principles, and strategies codified into teachings, writings, or institutions. A predator's offspring survive not just by instinct, but by inherited knowledge.
- **Impact Legacy**: Beyond wealth, apex dynasties shape industries, communities, and even nations. Like the fossil record, your influence becomes part of the landscape itself.

Multi-Generational Wealth: The Extinction-Proof Dynasty

The most powerful predators did not merely dominate their lifetime—they ensured their genetic survival across epochs. Wealth builders must do the same.

1. **Dynastic Structures**
    - Use trusts, holding companies, and family offices to consolidate wealth, prevent dilution, and create mechanisms for long-term growth.
2. **Wealth Education**
    - Teach heirs predator instincts. Many dynasties collapse because descendants are raised as passive prey instead of apex successors. Embed financial literacy, resilience, and entrepreneurial skills.
3. **Institutionalization of Power**
    - Foundations, universities, and corporations extend influence beyond family. Just as fossils define eras, institutions preserve dynastic dominance.
4. **Adaptability Across Generations**
    - Ensure your dynasty evolves with changing climates. Dinosaurs that could not adapt perished; dynasties that cling to outdated methods collapse. Build adaptive DNA into your legacy.

The Three Pillars of the Extinction-Proof Dynasty

1. **Eternal Assets**
    - Acquire assets that transcend eras: land, intellectual property, natural resources, and businesses with timeless relevance. These are your fossils, immune to short-term extinction events.
2. **Enduring Identity**
    - Establish a brand identity so strong that it carries through generations, like the Rockefeller or Rothschild names. These identities command respect long after their founders' deaths.
3. **Ecosystem Domination**
    - Position your dynasty at the center of industries, markets, or cultural spheres so that even in your absence, the ecosystem cannot function without your influence.

Case Studies: Dynasties That Became Extinction-Proof

- **The Rothschilds**: Banking and finance dominance structured across generations with adaptability baked in.
- **The Rockefellers**: Oil transformed into multi-industry wealth, protected by trusts and philanthropy.
- **The Disney Legacy**: Intellectual property transformed into an immortal cultural empire.
- **Modern Tech Dynasties**: Founders of Apple, Amazon, and Google who institutionalized innovation so their empires continue beyond them.

Each built more than wealth—they built **fossilized empires** that endure as part of civilization's fabric.

The Apex Predator's Final Evolution

The journey of the wealth predator ends not with a feast, but with an empire. You are no longer the hunter stalking prey. You are the **species that defines the ecosystem itself**. Every industry adapts to your presence. Every competitor measures themselves against you. Every descendant benefits from the fossils of wealth you leave behind.

The extinction-proof dynasty is not about your survival—it is about immortality. By building enduring assets, branding yourself into legend, and transferring predator instincts into future generations, you carve your wealth into stone.

Closing Pulse of Chapter Ten

Empires are not accidents. They are deliberate, patient constructions. The apex predator of wealth builds not for the season, nor even for the lifetime, but for the **ages**.

Your brand is your roar. Your legacy is your fossil. Your dynasty is your species' survival.

Others will vanish. Others will fade. But your empire, if built as extinction-proof, will outlive crises, markets, and even time itself.

To be an apex predator is to thrive.

To be an **apex empire builder** is to become immortal.

Final Epilogue – The Eternal Roar of the Dinosaur Mindset

The story of survival has always been written in teeth, claws, and bone. From the towering giants that thundered across prehistoric plains to the cunning mammals that darted through the shadows, life has always revolved around one law: **adapt or perish**. Dinosaurs may be gone, but their lessons are alive within us. Their fossils are more than remnants—they are monuments to dominance, reminders of both triumph and extinction, and eternal symbols of how power, timing, and resilience shape destiny.

You began this journey as prey in a modern jungle—a financial ecosystem designed to trap the unaware, the timid, and the passive. But as you've walked through these chapters, you have learned to shed the herd mentality, sharpen your instincts, and evolve into a predator of wealth. You have embraced adaptability, claimed territory, mastered timing, hunted in packs, stockpiled resources, unearthed rare fossils of enduring value, and positioned yourself at the top of the food chain.

Now you stand not merely as a survivor, but as something far greater—an **apex empire builder**.

The Arc of Transformation

1. **Survival** – Learning that wealth, like life, is not optional but a strategy.
2. **Dominance** – Seizing and defending territory, commanding ecosystems, and moving beyond dependence.
3. **Timing** – Striking when opportunity is ripe, refusing hesitation, and exploiting cycles of fear and greed.
4. **Alliances** – Harnessing the pack advantage, building networks, and multiplying force through cooperation.
5. **Cycles** – Thriving in abundance and scarcity, turning famine into opportunity and feast into preservation.
6. **Rare Assets** – Excavating the fossils of wealth: gold, land, intellectual property, and enduring legacies.
7. **Apex Positioning** – Rising to a level where your very presence defines the rules of the ecosystem.
8. **Empire Building** – Constructing the extinction-proof dynasty, branding your roar into eternity, and passing predator instincts to the generations that follow.

The Extinction-Proof Dynasty

Every creature that walked the earth faced extinction—but only some left fossils that shaped history. So too with wealth: money made and consumed vanishes; wealth fossilized into assets, brands, and dynasties endures.

The true predator does not measure success in years, but in **generations**. The extinction-proof dynasty is not about mere accumulation—it is about continuity. It is about creating systems, structures, and values that will protect your empire long after you are gone. It is about knowing that one day, when others dig through the fossils of this age, your name, your empire, and your roar will still be there.

Your Place in the New Age

You now possess the blueprint not only to survive this world, but to dominate it. The Dinosaur Mindset is not about nostalgia for a lost age—it is about remembering what evolution demands of us. Strength alone does not guarantee survival. Size does not guarantee dominance. But **adaptability, timing, resourcefulness, and foresight** ensure immortality.

As the financial jungles shift and asteroids of disruption strike, others will panic, scatter, or vanish. But you will not. You have learned the predator's patience, the hunter's ferocity, and the empire-builder's vision.

The Eternal Roar

One day, your life will end. That is inevitable. But whether your influence dies with you, or whether it roars across generations, is a choice. The Dinosaur Mindset has given you the tools to roar forever.

- Roar in your branding.
- Roar in your assets.
- Roar in your legacy.
- Roar in your dynasty.

When you are gone, let your wealth be the fossil that endures. Let your empire be the evidence that you were here. Let your roar be eternal.

The age of passive prey is over. The age of the predator has begun. But beyond the predator, beyond survival itself, lies something even greater: the eternal empire. And now—it is yours to build.

Appendix A – Jurassic Wealth Maps: Daily Rituals of the Richest Species

In the prehistoric wild, survival was not random. Every creature lived by patterns, rituals, and instincts that dictated whether they thrived or perished. Apex predators rose not because they were the strongest in one single moment, but because they repeated successful behaviors daily, honing instincts into habits.

Wealth follows the same law. Success is not built on one brilliant strike, one lucky investment, or one big opportunity—it is built on the **rituals you practice daily**. The richest "species" of modern wealth-builders cultivate behaviors that, over time, fossilize into dynasties.

This appendix is your **Jurassic Wealth Map**—a framework of predator-inspired daily rituals designed to align your instincts with compounding, extinction-proof success.

1. Morning Territory Patrol

Predator Equivalent: Apex hunters surveyed their territory each dawn, sensing prey, rivals, and shifts in the environment.

Wealth Ritual: Begin each day by scanning your financial ecosystem.

- Review accounts, assets, and investments briefly—know what has changed overnight.
- Read industry or market updates, scanning for threats and opportunities.
- Set your top three financial or strategic priorities for the day.

This practice establishes psychological dominance—you are not wandering blindly; you are **patrolling your domain**.

2. The Hunt Visualization

Predator Equivalent: Raptors coordinated the day's hunt before striking.

Wealth Ritual: Every morning, visualize the one "kill" you must make today.

- Ask: *What is the single action that will move my wealth forward today?*
- Examples: securing a client, making an investment decision, writing content, or finalizing a deal.
- Write it down and commit to completing it, no matter what distractions arise.

This channels energy into decisive strikes rather than scattered effort.

3. The Pack Communication Ritual

Predator Equivalent: Raptors thrived by signaling and communicating within the pack.

Wealth Ritual: Strengthen alliances daily.

- Send one message, email, or call to an ally, mentor, or partner.
- Share intelligence or create opportunities that reinforce bonds.
- Expand your network intentionally: at least one new meaningful connection per week.

Your wealth pack must be fed as consistently as your assets.

4. Scarcity and Abundance Journaling

Predator Equivalent: Survivors stored resources in feast and rationed them in famine.

Wealth Ritual: Train your psychology to thrive in both cycles.

- Write down one way you conserved resources today.
- Write down one way you invested, grew, or expanded today.

This balance ritual ensures you are never reckless in abundance nor paralyzed in scarcity.

5. The Fossil Excavation Practice

Predator Equivalent: Some creatures survived by burrowing, digging, and caching treasures beneath the earth.

Wealth Ritual: Spend 20–30 minutes daily on **deep digging for rare assets**.

- Research undervalued opportunities (real estate, intellectual property, rare markets).
- Revisit long-term plays that others overlook.
- Add one idea or asset candidate to your "fossil vault" journal weekly.

This ensures your dynasty is built on rare, enduring treasures—not fleeting prey.

6. Predator Fitness and Discipline

Predator Equivalent: The strongest hunters maintained their power through daily movement and ritual behaviors.

Wealth Ritual: Train your body and mind for endurance.

- Commit to 30 minutes of physical movement daily (walk, stretch, train).
- Practice mental clarity rituals (meditation, visualization, or focused breathing).
- Guard your diet and rest as fiercely as your bank account.

Wealth predators cannot dominate with weak health; energy is the fuel of empire.

7. Daily Resource Allocation

Predator Equivalent: Successful hunters conserved energy and targeted the most rewarding prey.

Wealth Ritual: End each day with deliberate resource management.

- Allocate surplus: decide how much of today's income or profit will be stored, invested, or reinvested.
- Track savings, debt reduction, and investments consistently.
- Ask: *Did I grow my reserves today, or did I consume them?*

This creates an unbreakable rhythm of compounding wealth.

8. Evening Fossilization Ritual

Predator Equivalent: Fossils are legacies of what endured. Each day leaves its trace.

Wealth Ritual: Document your daily footprint.

- Write down what worked today, what failed, and what you learned.
- Capture one decision that will matter years from now.
- End with gratitude—predators who survived the day celebrated survival.

Over time, this journal becomes your personal fossil record of wealth-building.

The Predator's 24-Hour Map

Morning:

- Patrol territory (scan finances + markets).
- Visualize today's hunt.
- Strengthen pack ties.

Daytime:

- Execute the one "kill" (high-priority wealth action).
- Excavate rare opportunities (deep research).
- Train body and mind.

Evening:

- Allocate resources (save/invest).
- Fossilize the day's lessons (journal).

Closing Pulse of Appendix A

The richest species were not those who struck once—they were those who **ritualized survival into dominance**. Wealth is built the same way. These Jurassic Wealth Maps transform instinct into structure, structure into habits, and habits into dynasties.

Repeat these daily rituals, and you will no longer chase wealth blindly. You will live as a predator of fortune, compounding power until your empire becomes inevitable.

Each day you follow this map, you are not just surviving—you are writing your fossil record, one that will echo through generations.

Appendix B – Predator Wealth Tools & Practices

In the prehistoric jungle, apex predators didn't simply rely on brute strength. They relied on tools nature had given them—keen senses, sharp claws, powerful jaws, and instinctive tactics. These weren't random gifts; they were survival technologies, refined over millions of years. In wealth, the same law applies. To thrive as a modern predator, you must arm yourself with the right **tools** and sharpen the right **practices**. Without them, your instincts are blunted, and your empire risks collapse before it matures.

This appendix outlines the arsenal every wealth predator requires: practical financial tools, proven strategies, and daily practices that translate prehistoric instincts into modern dominance.

1. The Predator's Vision Tools

Equivalent: Keen eyesight of raptors, night vision of nocturnal hunters, sensitivity to movement.

Wealth Translation: Tools that give you visibility into your ecosystem.

- **Financial Dashboards**: Use apps or platforms (e.g., YNAB, Mint, Personal Capital) to track all accounts, investments, debts, and cash flow at a glance.
- **Market Radars**: Follow key financial indicators daily (interest rates, market indexes, inflation data). Build a watchlist of industries, stocks, or assets tied to your niche.
- **Trend Tracking**: Use Google Trends, newsletters, and data platforms to sense emerging industries before the herd sees them.

Practice: Spend 15 minutes each morning surveying your "territory." Like a predator scanning for prey, this keeps you alert to threats and opportunities.

2. The Claws and Teeth of Finance

Equivalent: A predator's ability to strike and finish the kill.

Wealth Translation: Instruments and vehicles that allow you to take decisive financial action.

- **Brokerage Accounts**: For striking quickly in equities, ETFs, and options.
- **Alternative Investment Platforms**: For access to real estate syndicates, startups, or private equity.
- **Precious Metals and Hard Assets**: Gold, silver, or commodities as claws against inflation and uncertainty.
- **Legal Entities**: LLCs, corporations, and trusts to protect assets, minimize taxes, and separate personal from business risk.

Practice: Predators don't hesitate. When prey is vulnerable, they strike. Train yourself to act decisively when conditions match your criteria.

3. The Camouflage and Armor Layer

Equivalent: Thick hides, camouflage, or defensive spines.
**Wealth Translation: Tools that protect you from predators (banks, governments, rivals).*

- **Insurance Shields**: Health, disability, and liability coverage to prevent financial collapse from sudden attacks.
- **Asset Protection**: Trusts, offshore accounts, and legal structuring that shield wealth from lawsuits and creditors.
- **Tax Strategy Armor**: Work with advisors or use tax software to create structures that reduce exposure while maximizing reinvestment potential.

Practice: Review your defenses quarterly. Predators are vulnerable when they overhunt without protection—ensure your armor is strong before expanding.

4. The Pack Communication Tools
Equivalent: Raptors' signals and wolf howls.
* *Wealth Translation: Networking and relationship-building systems.*

- **CRM Systems** (Customer Relationship Management): Track leads, clients, and partners.
- **Networking Platforms**: LinkedIn, masterminds, investment groups, and alliances that share intelligence.
- **Mentorship Channels**: Systems for learning from predators above you in the food chain.

Practice: Commit to one meaningful pack interaction daily (call, message, collaboration). The predator without a pack has fewer eyes to spot prey and fewer allies to defend its territory.

5. The Hoarding and Caching Systems

Equivalent: Crocodiles storing fat, mammals burying food, birds migrating with reserves.
* *Wealth Translation: Systems that preserve and grow your reserves.*

- **Emergency Funds**: Liquid cash equal to 6–12 months of survival.
- **Automated Savings Systems**: Accounts that receive a percentage of all income before it is spent.
- **Investment Automations**: Scheduled contributions to index funds, retirement accounts, or long-term assets.
- **Storage Vaults**: Diversified repositories (banks, brokerage, vaults, digital wallets).

Practice: Automate hoarding. Set systems that stash away wealth without requiring daily decision-making. Predators don't debate survival—they ritualize it.

6. The Hunting Playbook

Equivalent: Patterns of stalking, ambushing, and chasing prey.
**Wealth Translation: Step-by-step frameworks that guide financial strikes.*

- **Opportunity Screens**: Write criteria for what makes an investment "prey-worthy" (risk level, ROI, alignment with long-term goals).
- **Checklists for Action**: Before a strike, review: Does this fit my ecosystem? Does it strengthen my dynasty?
- **Exit Plans**: Predators don't chase prey endlessly. Set rules for when to exit investments, businesses, or partnerships.

Practice: Refine and rehearse your playbook weekly. The best predators succeed not because they improvise but because they have repeatable, lethal systems.

7. The Fossilization Tools

Equivalent: Fossils that preserve dominance for millions of years.
* *Wealth Translation: Systems for converting temporary wins into permanent dynasties.*

- **Trusts and Foundations**: Fossilize wealth by protecting it beyond your lifetime.
- **Intellectual Property Registration**: Secure patents, copyrights, and trademarks as fossils of thought.
- **Succession Planning**: Educate heirs, codify principles, and build frameworks to transfer predator instincts across generations.

Practice: Every year, ask: *If I vanished today, would my empire fossilize or collapse?* If collapse is the answer, rebuild your structures until they endure without you.

8. The Predator Mind Rituals

Equivalent: Daily instincts honed through repetition.

* *Wealth Translation: Mental and behavioral practices that sustain dominance.*

- **Morning Ecosystem Scan**: As outlined in Appendix A, patrol your domain daily.
- **Kill Focus**: One high-value wealth action per day.
- **Reflection Journal**: Fossilize lessons, ensuring each failure evolves into strength.
- **Abundance/Scarcity Awareness**: End the day by recording how you stored and how you grew.

Practice: Wealth predators thrive on **discipline**. Rituals turn instincts into dynasties.

Closing Pulse of Appendix B

Predators ruled prehistory not because they were the biggest or strongest, but because they wielded the right tools in the right way. Wealth predators must do the same. Your claws are your contracts, your armor is your legal structure, your camouflage is your discretion, and your fossils are the assets you pass down.

The herd wanders, the scavenger waits, but the predator strikes with precision—armed, armored, and prepared. With these tools and practices, you are no longer at the mercy of financial ecosystems. You are the one shaping them, ensuring your dynasty becomes not only dominant but **extinction-proof**.

Appendix C – The Extinction Barriers: Mistakes That Kill Dynasties Before They Begin

In the fossil record, the story of failure is written as clearly as the story of dominance. For every mighty predator that ruled its ecosystem, countless species perished before they could adapt, evolve, or establish lasting survival strategies. Some grew too large for the food supply. Others relied on fragile ecosystems that collapsed. Still others ignored the subtle signals of coming disaster until it was too late.

Wealth works no differently. For every dynasty that thrives across generations, dozens collapse before they even begin. Some are destroyed by greed, others by fear, others by ignorance of the cycles that govern the financial ecosystem. This appendix outlines the **extinction barriers**—the fatal mistakes that eliminate wealth predators before their empires can fossilize into legacy.

1. The Illusion of Endless Abundance

Prehistoric Lesson: Dinosaurs overgrazed and overhunted when prey was plentiful, leaving themselves vulnerable when scarcity struck.

Wealth Mistake: Believing bull markets, booming careers, or high profits will last forever.

- Overspending in times of plenty.
- Expanding businesses too rapidly without reserves.
- Ignoring the inevitability of recessions and crises.

Predator Practice: Always prepare for scarcity during abundance. Set aside reserves, diversify assets, and assume every feast has an expiration date.

2. The Fossilized Mindset

Prehistoric Lesson: Species that could not adapt to new climates or food sources vanished.

Wealth Mistake: Refusing to evolve strategies, skills, or investments.

- Sticking with outdated industries or jobs long after they decline.
- Ignoring technology shifts (AI, digital platforms, renewable energy).
- Assuming what worked for one generation will work for the next.

Predator Practice: Keep learning. Rotate prey trails. Evolve skill sets and investment approaches with every new economic season.

3. The Lone Wolf Delusion

Prehistoric Lesson: Raptors thrived in packs; solitary hunters often fell to larger rivals.

Wealth Mistake: Trying to build wealth entirely alone.

- Refusing partnerships, mentorship, or alliances.
- Rejecting feedback or guidance.
- Believing independence means isolation.

Predator Practice: Build your pack. Networks, advisors, and mentors increase your survival odds and multiply opportunity.

4. The Overexpansion Trap

Prehistoric Lesson: Some giant dinosaurs grew too large, requiring massive amounts of food; when ecosystems shifted, their size doomed them.
Wealth Mistake: Expanding too fast without sustainability.

- Scaling businesses or portfolios faster than cash flow supports.
- Taking on excessive debt or leverage.
- Building empires without defensive structures (legal, tax, savings).

Predator Practice: Grow with balance. Expansion should strengthen, not weaken, your ecosystem. Test stability before scaling.

5. The Fear Paralysis

Prehistoric Lesson: Prey animals frozen in fear became easy kills.

Wealth Mistake: Hesitating to act when opportunities are ripe.

- Waiting for "perfect timing" and missing the strike.
- Avoiding risks entirely, guaranteeing mediocrity.
- Freezing during crises instead of acting decisively.

Predator Practice: Courage in scarcity is wealth's greatest ally. Train reflexes to strike when conditions align—even if fear whispers otherwise.

6. The Scavenger Mentality

Prehistoric Lesson: Scavengers survived, but never dominated. They fed on scraps left by true predators.

Wealth Mistake: Living entirely off leftover opportunities.

- Following the herd into bubbles.
- Chasing trends only after they peak.
- Settling for low-value scraps instead of hunting for high-value kills.

Predator Practice: Hunt proactively. Seek undervalued, overlooked, or emerging opportunities before the herd arrives.

7. The Dynasty Drain

Prehistoric Lesson: Even survivors perished if their offspring lacked survival instincts.

Wealth Mistake: Building wealth but failing to pass predator instincts to heirs.

- Giving wealth without guidance.
- Allowing inheritance to create weak, entitled descendants.
- Lacking succession structures (trusts, foundations, or businesses designed for continuity).

Predator Practice: Educate heirs in predator discipline. Build structures that enforce sustainability and responsibility. Wealth without wisdom leads to collapse.

8. The Armor Neglect

Prehistoric Lesson: Creatures without defenses were picked off easily.

Wealth Mistake: Failing to protect wealth from external predators.

- No insurance, no asset protection, no legal safeguards.
- Vulnerability to lawsuits, taxes, or market predators.
- Visibility without defensive camouflage.

Predator Practice: Protect first, expand second. Build moats—trusts, entities, insurance—before exposing your empire to the ecosystem.

9. The Short-Sighted Hunt

Prehistoric Lesson: Predators that chased every small prey exhausted themselves and missed bigger opportunities.
Wealth Mistake: Prioritizing short-term gratification over long-term wealth.

- Spending profits instead of reinvesting.
- Obsessing over quick flips, ignoring long-term assets.
- Failing to fossilize wealth into enduring assets (land, IP, legacy).

Predator Practice: Balance daily kills with fossil building. Feed today, but always fossilize for tomorrow.

10. The Complacency Collapse

Prehistoric Lesson: Apex predators that stopped adapting were eventually outcompeted or destroyed by environmental shifts.

Wealth Mistake: Believing success guarantees permanence.

- Ignoring competition.
- Failing to innovate after achieving dominance.
- Assuming wealth will manage itself.

Predator Practice: Stay vigilant. The predator that stops hunting becomes prey. Empire maintenance is daily, not optional.

The Extinction Equation

Extinction occurs when these barriers combine: **greed in abundance + fear in scarcity + refusal to adapt + lack of defense.** This equation has killed countless dynasties. The herd dies from blindness. The scavenger dies from scraps. The predator who ignores barriers dies from arrogance.

Closing Pulse of Appendix C

The fossil record teaches us as much about failure as it does about dominance. The creatures that vanished before their time serve as eternal warnings: survival requires vigilance. Wealth is no different. Dynasties are not destroyed by chance—they are destroyed by mistakes repeated until collapse is inevitable.

If you avoid these extinction barriers, your empire will endure. If you master the predator practices outlined in this book, your dynasty will fossilize into history.

The choice is yours:

Will your wealth vanish as another forgotten species?

Or will your empire become the **extinction-proof dynasty**, a fossilized legacy echoing through the ages?

Appendix D – The Apex Predator's Wealth Timeline: A Step-by-Step Evolution Plan

In the prehistoric world, no predator began life as an apex force. The Tyrannosaurus hatched as a vulnerable hatchling. Raptors began as small, fragile creatures, dependent on the pack for safety. Only through stages of growth, testing, and adaptation did they rise to the top of their ecosystems.

Wealth evolution follows the same law. You do not leap from prey to apex predator overnight. Instead, you move through **progressive stages of survival, hunting, and empire-building**, each requiring new skills, tools, and instincts. Skip a stage, and you risk collapse. Master each stage, and you ascend the food chain until your wealth becomes an empire.

This appendix maps the **Apex Predator's Wealth Timeline**—a step-by-step evolutionary plan designed to guide you from vulnerability to extinction-proof dynasty.

Stage One – Prey Survival (The Vulnerable Hatchling)

Identity: Dependent, exposed, learning.

Goal: Escape financial vulnerability and secure survival basics.

Core Challenges:

- Living paycheck to paycheck.
- Reliance on a single income source.
- High debt exposure and no reserves.

Predator Practices:

1. **Escape Immediate Danger:** Build a basic emergency fund (1–3 months of expenses).
2. **Reduce Debt Predators:** Pay down high-interest debt that drains resources.
3. **Secure Shelter:** Stabilize housing, food, and healthcare before attempting empire building.

Milestone to Advance: Achieve financial stability where survival is no longer threatened by a single unexpected event.

Stage Two – The Scavenger Phase (Learning to Feed)

Identity: Opportunist, feeding on scraps, beginning to learn the hunt.

Goal: Build initial wealth by leveraging what others ignore.

Core Challenges:

- Limited capital.
- Following trends rather than creating them.
- Relying on secondary opportunities.

Predator Practices:

1. **Side Income Scraps:** Start side hustles, freelance work, or micro-investments to test new food sources.
2. **Scavenger's Intelligence:** Learn from mentors, books, and courses—take advantage of knowledge others leave behind.
3. **Begin Hoarding:** Start building 6–12 months of emergency reserves.

Milestone to Advance: Create multiple income streams and accumulate a foundation of savings to reduce dependency on the herd.

Stage Three – The Hunter Phase (First Blood)

Identity: Independent predator, striking small prey.

Goal: Begin targeted wealth creation through deliberate action.

Core Challenges:

- Lack of confidence in timing.
- Risk of missed strikes or failed hunts.
- Overreliance on one strategy.

Predator Practices:

1. **Target Small Prey:** Make calculated investments in stocks, real estate, or small business ventures.
2. **Refine the Kill:** Learn entry and exit strategies—avoid chasing every opportunity.
3. **Create Hunting Rituals:** Daily financial tracking, weekly reviews, monthly strategy updates.

Milestone to Advance: Consistent wealth growth through active hunting, not just scavenging.

Stage Four – The Pack Predator Phase (Coordinated Hunts)

Identity: Team hunter, multiplying power through alliances.
Goal: Use networks and collaborations to secure larger prey.

Core Challenges:

- Choosing the wrong allies.
- Trust breakdowns or unequal profit-sharing.
- Risk of groupthink.

Predator Practices:

1. **Form Wealth Packs:** Join syndicates, partnerships, or investment groups.
2. **Leverage Collective Intelligence:** Share leads, research, and opportunities within the pack.
3. **Secure Larger Kills:** Acquire rental properties, invest in startups, or launch scalable businesses.

Milestone to Advance: Demonstrate the ability to multiply returns by leveraging alliances while maintaining trust and boundaries.

Stage Five – Apex Predator Positioning (Dominance in Territory)

Identity: Recognized leader, feared and respected in the ecosystem. *Goal:* Build visibility, authority, and control in chosen niches.

Core Challenges:

- Overconfidence leading to overexpansion.
- Attracting rivals and predators.
- Balancing scale with defense.

Predator Practices:

1. **Claim Territory:** Dominate a niche or industry until your name becomes synonymous with it.
2. **Build Moats:** Protect wealth through legal structures, intellectual property, and reputation.
3. **Control Ecosystems:** Position yourself at the center of supply chains, customer flows, or financial networks.

Milestone to Advance: Your presence shifts industries. You no longer chase wealth; opportunities seek you.

Stage Six – Empire Builder (The Apex Civilization)

Identity: Architect of legacy.

Goal: Fossilize wealth into dynasties that survive beyond your lifetime.

Core Challenges:

- Entropy across generations.
- Loss of predator instinct in heirs.
- Complacency in abundance.

Predator Practices:

1. **Fossilization of Wealth:** Convert profits into enduring assets (land, gold, IP, businesses with moats).
2. **Dynastic Structures:** Establish trusts, family offices, and succession plans.
3. **Teach Predator DNA:** Embed financial literacy, adaptability, and resilience into the next generation.
4. **Institutionalize the Empire:** Foundations, charities, or global initiatives that make your name immortal.

Milestone to Advance: Your dynasty operates and thrives without your presence. The wealth ecosystem cannot ignore your legacy.

The Apex Predator's Timeline at a Glance

1. **Prey Survival** – Escape financial vulnerability.
2. **Scavenger Phase** – Build stability with scraps and small wins.
3. **Hunter Phase** – Take deliberate, targeted financial strikes.
4. **Pack Predator Phase** – Multiply results through alliances.
5. **Apex Predator Positioning** – Dominate niches, control ecosystems.
6. **Empire Builder** – Fossilize wealth into extinction-proof dynasties.

Closing Pulse of Appendix D

Wealth is not a sprint to dominance—it is an **evolutionary climb**. Each stage builds on the last, requiring new instincts, tools, and practices. Skip stages, and your empire collapses like an overgrown dinosaur unable to feed itself. Master each stage, and you rise until your roar echoes across generations.

The Apex Predator's Wealth Timeline is not just a plan—it is a **map of evolution**. Follow it, and your wealth will not only survive the asteroids of disruption but will fossilize into a dynasty that outlives extinction itself.

Appendix E – The Predator's Daily Strike Plan: A Step-by-Step Action Blueprint

In prehistory, apex predators did not survive by chance. They survived because every day followed a sequence of instinctive actions—scanning, stalking, striking, and securing resources. Each step was part of a rhythm, refined over millions of years. If a predator skipped even one step, it risked hunger, vulnerability, or death.

Wealth works the same way. Without daily structure, ambition dissolves into distraction, and opportunity slips past. This appendix is your **Predator's Daily Strike Plan**—a tactical checklist that translates prehistoric hunting patterns into actionable modern wealth-building rituals. By following it, you align every day with the predator's evolutionary path: survival → dominance → dynasty.

Step 1: Dawn Patrol – Survey Your Territory

Prehistoric Equivalent: Predators waking at first light to scan the land for prey and threats.

Action Blueprint:

- **Review Finances**: Check balances, cash flow, and outstanding obligations.
- **Scan the Ecosystem**: Read quick updates on markets, industries, or news affecting your niche.
- **Mark Your Territory**: Write down your *top three wealth priorities* for the day.

Purpose: Begin the day as a ruler, not as prey. Awareness establishes control.

Step 2: The Hunt Target – Choose Today's Kill
Prehistoric Equivalent: Raptors coordinating which prey to stalk.
Action Blueprint:

- Select one high-impact action that will move your wealth forward (e.g., closing a deal, launching content, investing, prospecting).
- Write it as your **"Kill of the Day."**
- Commit to finishing it no matter what distractions arise.

Purpose: Predators don't chase everything. They strike one decisive blow.

Step 3: Pack Communication – Strengthen Alliances

Prehistoric Equivalent: Predator packs signaling before the hunt.

Action Blueprint:

- Reach out to **one ally, partner, or mentor** to maintain strong pack bonds.
- Share value: send an insight, opportunity, or introduction.
- Expand: connect with one new potential ally per week.

Purpose: A strong pack multiplies your hunting power and intelligence.

Step 4: Midday Strike – Execute with Precision

Prehistoric Equivalent: The predator's ambush, executed with timing and force.

Action Blueprint:

- Block 1–3 hours in the day for deep, undistracted work on your "Kill of the Day."
- Remove distractions (no email, social media, or idle browsing).
- Execute with predator focus until the strike is complete.

Purpose: Wealth is built not in scattered activity but in decisive, focused strikes.

Step 5: Resource Allocation – Feed and Store

Prehistoric Equivalent: After the hunt, predators fed and hid leftovers from scavengers.

Action Blueprint:

- Allocate a percentage of income from the day into three categories:
  1. **Consumption** (basic needs, survival).
  2. **Storage** (savings, reserves, defensive cash).
  3. **Growth** (investments, business reinvestment).
- Automate this process as much as possible.

Purpose: Never consume everything you kill. Always stash and grow.

Step 6: Fossil Excavation – Dig for Long-Term Assets

Prehistoric Equivalent: Creatures burrowing or caching resources underground for future survival.

Action Blueprint:

- Spend 20–30 minutes daily researching **rare, enduring opportunities** (land, IP, gold, undervalued markets).
- Add findings to your "Fossil Vault Journal."
- Set weekly targets: at least one new potential long-term asset identified.

Purpose: Daily digs create tomorrow's fossils—assets that outlast you.

Step 7: Predator Fitness – Sharpen the Body and Mind

Prehistoric Equivalent: The strongest predators thrived through agility, endurance, and health.

Action Blueprint:

- Move: minimum 30 minutes of physical training, walking, or stretching.
- Mental clarity: meditation, visualization, or breathwork to reset instincts.
- Nutrition: eat for energy, not comfort.

Purpose: A weak predator cannot hunt. Health is the first empire.

Step 8: Scarcity/Abundance Journal – Cycle Awareness

Prehistoric Equivalent: Animals adjusting to seasonal shifts.

Action Blueprint:

- Write one line each day on how you **conserved** (scarcity mindset).
- Write one line each day on how you **expanded** (abundance mindset).
- This trains you to thrive in both cycles, never trapped by one.

Purpose: Awareness of cycles prevents extinction.

Step 9: Evening Fossilization – Record the Day's Lessons

Prehistoric Equivalent: Fossils recording life in stone for ages to come.

Action Blueprint:

- Write down what worked, what failed, and one lesson learned today.
- Capture one decision or action that will matter in 1–5 years.
- End with gratitude for survival and progress.

Purpose: Daily fossilization transforms experience into wisdom that compounds.

Step 10: Rest and Reset – Predator Stillness

Prehistoric Equivalent: Predators conserved energy between hunts, resting to strike again tomorrow.

Action Blueprint:

- Disconnect from work at a set time to preserve mental reserves.
- Prioritize 7–8 hours of restorative sleep.
- End with a mental reset ritual: visualization of tomorrow's hunt.

Purpose: Even the fiercest predator starves without energy for the next strike.

The Predator's Daily Strike Checklist

Morning:
◈ Territory patrol (finances + market scan)
◈ Identify "Kill of the Day"
◈ Strengthen one alliance

Daytime:
◈ Execute "Kill of the Day" (deep work block)
◈ Allocate resources: consume/store/grow
◈ Fossil excavation research
◈ Predator fitness (body + mind training)

Evening:
◈ Scarcity/abundance journal entry
◈ Fossilize the day's lessons
◈ Rest + reset for tomorrow's hunt

Closing Pulse of Appendix E

Predators thrive not because of luck but because of **ritualized behavior**. Each day, they follow an instinctive blueprint: scan, strike, feed, store, and rest. Wealth predators who follow this daily plan transform survival into dominance, and dominance into dynasty.

When you repeat this strike plan, wealth-building stops being a dream and becomes your biology—etched into your instincts like the roars of ancient hunters. Each day becomes a fossil, each fossil becomes a record, and together they form the **extinction-proof empire** that outlives you.

Appendix F – The Apex Predator's Survival Questions

At the top of the evolutionary chain, survival is no longer about escaping extinction alone—it is about thriving, adapting, and remaining untouchable. But predators who stop questioning themselves eventually fall prey to stagnation, overconfidence, or environmental changes they never anticipated.

This final appendix is your **self-interrogation manual**—a set of survival questions designed to keep you sharp, alert, and always ahead of the prey (and the other predators). Use these questions as daily, weekly, and yearly reflections. They will force you to test your assumptions, sharpen your instincts, and refine your empire-building strategies.

Think of this as the **"roar before the hunt"**—the moment you ensure you are fully aligned before striking into the financial wilds.

Section I: Daily Survival Questions – The Predator's Morning Scan

Every day begins with a hunt. These questions sharpen your daily awareness:

1. **Where is today's prey?**
   – What single activity, deal, or opportunity will bring me the highest return today?
2. **Am I alert or distracted?**
   – What mental clutter needs clearing before I go on the hunt?
3. **Is my environment favorable?**
   – Are the markets, my networks, or my physical health aligned for today's strike?
4. **What do I need to kill off?**
   – Which task, habit, or relationship is draining energy that should fuel growth?
5. **Who in my pack do I need to empower today?**
   – Which alliance member, partner, or employee should be strengthened for long-term advantage?
6. **Am I moving fast enough?**
   – Is there a window of opportunity today that will close if I hesitate?
7. **What is the fallback plan if the hunt fails?**
   – Do I have a backup source of momentum if today's prey escapes?

Predator's Ritual: Write these answers each morning in a survival journal before you begin your work. This builds instinctive clarity.

Section II: Weekly Questions – The Pack and Territory Audit

Every seven days, the apex predator zooms out. These questions ensure you're not trapped in short-term skirmishes:

1. **Did I expand or lose territory this week?**
   – Did I secure new clients, markets, or resources—or did competitors push me back?
2. **Who in my pack strengthened me, and who weakened me?**
   – Are alliances balanced, or am I carrying dead weight?
3. **Did I act too much like the herd?**
   – Where did I follow trends instead of setting them?
4. **What patterns of prey did I notice?**
   – Are new consumer needs, trends, or gaps emerging?
5. **What fossilized habits am I still clinging to?**
   – Which outdated strategies are dragging me down?
6. **What apex move did I make?**
   – Did I do something this week that positioned me as a species others cannot ignore?

Predator's Ritual: Every Sunday night, journal answers, extract one critical shift for the next week, and design one apex move for the days ahead.

Section III: Monthly Questions – Seasonal Survival & Scarcity Readiness

At the end of each month, predators check resource levels, migration paths, and predator-prey balance.

1. **Am I prepared for seasonal shifts?**
   – Am I building reserves for the inevitable scarcity season?
2. **Is my resource hoarding balanced?**
   – Do I have enough liquid assets for survival and enough long-term assets for dynastic growth?
3. **What new bones did I dig up?**
   – Did I uncover rare opportunities, undervalued investments, or intellectual property?
4. **Who is circling me?**
   – Are competitors, regulations, or disruptive technologies approaching my hunting grounds?
5. **What part of my empire grew this month?**
   – Revenue, branding, alliances, or influence—where did expansion happen?
6. **Where am I vulnerable?**
   – Did I expose myself to unnecessary risks, debts, or predators stronger than me?

Predator's Ritual: Close every month with a financial audit and answer these questions before setting next month's strike strategy.

Section IV: Annual Survival Questions – Apex Dynasty Review

Once per year, the predator must take stock of its entire ecosystem. This is the dynasty check—your safeguard against slow extinction.

1. **Did my empire grow, stagnate, or shrink this year?**
   – Not just financially—did my influence, alliances, and brand grow?
2. **Do I control my territory—or am I merely surviving in it?**
   – Am I dictating the terms of the game, or reacting to others' moves?
3. **Am I leaving a fossil record worth studying?**
   – Will my wealth strategies be remembered, imitated, or ignored?
4. **Who will inherit my hunting grounds if I fall?**
   – Is my dynasty extinction-proof, or am I just rich in this generation?
5. **What predators rose this year that I must watch?**
   – Who emerged stronger that might challenge my apex position?
6. **What prey species are disappearing?**
   – Am I hunting markets or opportunities that are going extinct?
7. **What did I fail to adapt to?**
   – Which technologies, ideas, or strategies did I ignore at my peril?
8. **Did I act like prey anywhere in my empire?**
   – Where did fear, hesitation, or indecision weaken my position?

Predator's Ritual: Conduct this audit during the final week of the year. Use answers to set your dynasty's 10-year trajectory.

Section V: The Extinction-Proof Dynasty Check – The Final Five Questions

These ultimate questions define whether you remain apex or collapse into fossils:

1. **If I died tomorrow, would my dynasty survive without me?**
2. **Am I building wealth that multiplies without my direct hunting effort?**
3. **Do I have an empire strong enough to outlast economic winters, technological shifts, and political storms?**
4. **Will my name echo through financial history as apex—or be forgotten?**
5. **Have I built something so resilient that predators unborn will study me, not just out of respect, but envy?**

Closing Words of Appendix F

The predator who keeps asking survival questions never softens into prey. Every question above is a mirror, forcing you to confront weakness before the world does.

The dinosaurs that ruled the Earth once thought they were eternal. The only difference between them and you is **self-awareness**.

Ask, adapt, and advance—because extinction waits for those who stop questioning.

Message from the Author:

I hope you enjoyed this book, I love astrology and knew there was not a book such as this out on the shelf. I love metaphysical items as well. Please check out my other books:

-Life of Government Benefits

-My life of Hell

-My life with Hydrocephalus

-Red Sky

-World Domination:Woman's rule

-World Domination:Woman's Rule 2: The War

-Life and Banishment of Apophis: book 1

-The Kidney Friendly Diet

-The Ultimate Hemp Cookbook

-Creating a Dispensary(legally)

-Cleanliness throughout life: the importance of showering from childhood to adulthood.

-Strong Roots: The Risks of Overcoddling children

-Hemp Horoscopes: Cosmic Insights and Earthly Healing

- Celestial Hemp Navigating the Zodiac: Through the Green Cosmos

-Astrological Hemp: Aligning The Stars with Earth's Ancient Herb

-The Astrological Guide to Hemp: Stars, Signs, and Sacred Leaves

-Green Growth: Innovative Marketing Strategies for your Hemp Products and Dispensary

-Cosmic Cannabis

-Astrological Munchies

-Henry The Hemp

-Zodiacal Roots: The Astrological Soul Of Hemp

- **Green Constellations: Intersection of Hemp and Zodiac**

-Hemp in The Houses: An astrological Adventure Through The Cannabis Galaxy

-Galactic Ganja Guide
Heavenly Hemp
Zodiac Leaves
Doctor Who Astrology
Cannastrology
Stellar Satvias and Cosmic Indicas
Celestial Cannabis: A Zodiac Journey
AstroHerbology: The Sky and The Soil: Volume 1
AstroHerbology:Celestial Cannabis:Volume 2
Cosmic Cannabis Cultivation
The Starry Guide to Herbal Harmony: Volume 1
The Starry Guide to Herbal Harmony: Cannabis Universe: Volume 2
Yugioh Astrology: Astrological Guide to Deck, Duels and more
Nightmare Mansion: Echoes of The Abyss
Nightmare Mansion 2: Legacy of Shadows
Nightmare Mansion 3: Shadows of the Forgotten
Nightmare Mansion 4: Echoes of the Damned
The Life and Banishment of Apophis: Book 2
Nightmare Mansion: Halls of Despair
Healing with Herb: Cannabis and Hydrocephalus
Planetary Pot: Aligning with Astrological Herbs: Volume 1
Fast Track to Freedom: 30 Days to Financial Independence Using AI, Assets, and Agile Hustles
Cosmic Hemp Pathways
How to Become Financially Free in 30 Days: 10,000 Paths to Prosperity
Zodiacal Herbage: Astrological Insights: Volume 1
Nightmare Mansion: Whispers in the Walls
The Daleks Invade Atlantis
Henry the hemp and Hydrocephalus

10X The Kidney Friendly Diet
Cannabis Universe: Adult coloring book
Hemp Astrology: The Healing Power of the Stars
Zodiacal Herbage: Astrological Insights: Cannabis Universe: Volume 2
Planetary Pot: Aligning with Astrological Herbs: Cannabis Universes: Volume 2
Doctor Who: Convergence Protocol – The Replicator War
Nightmare Mansion: Curse of the Blood Moon
The Celestial Stoner: A Guide to the Zodiac
Cosmic Pleasures: Sex Toy Astrology for Every Sign
Hydrocephalus Astrology: Navigating the Stars and Healing Waters
Lapis and the Mischievous Chocolate Bar

Celestial Positions: Sexual Astrology for Every Sign
Apophis's Shadow Work Journal: **:** A Journey of Self-Discovery and Healing
Kinky Cosmos: Sexual Kink Astrology for Every Sign
Digital Cosmos: The Astrological Digimon Compendium
Stellar Seeds: The Cosmic Guide to Growing with Astrology
Apophis's Daily Gratitude Journal

Cat Astrology: Feline Mysteries of the Cosmos
The Cosmic Kama Sutra: An Astrological Guide to Sexual Positions
Unleash Your Potential: A Guided Journal Powered by AI Insights
Whispers of the Enchanted Grove

Cosmic Pleasures: An Astrological Guide to Sexual Kinks
369, 12 Manifestation Journal

Whisper of the nocturne journal(blank journal for writing or drawing)

The Boogey Book

Locked In Reflection: A Chastity Journey Through Locktober

Generating Wealth Quickly:How to Generate $100,000 in 24 Hours

Star Magic: Harness the Power of the Universe

The Flatulence Chronicles: A Fart Journal for Self-Discovery

The Doctor and The Death Moth

Seize the Day: A Personal Seizure Tracking Journal

The Ultimate Boogeyman Safari: A Journey into the Boogie World and Beyond

Whispers of Samhain: 1,000 Spells of Love, Luck, and Lunar Magic: Samhain Spell Book

Apophis's guides:Witch's Spellbook Crafting Guide for Halloween

Frost & Flame: The Enchanted Yule Grimoire of 1000 Winter Spells

The Ultimate Boogey Goo Guide & Spooky Activities for Halloween Fun

Harmony of the Scales: A Libra's Spellcraft for Balance and Beauty

The Enchanted Advent: 36 Days of Christmas Wonders

Nightmare Mansion: The Labyrinth of Screams

Harvest of Enchantment: 1,000 Spells of Gratitude, Love, and Fortune for Thanksgiving

The Boogey Chronicles: A Journal of Nightly Encounters and Shadowy Secrets

The 12 Days of Financial Freedom: A Step-by-Step Christmas Countdown to Transform Your Finances

Sigil of the Eternal Spiral Blank Journal

A Christmas Feast: Timeless Recipes for Every Meal

Holiday Stress-Free Solutions: A Survival Guide to Thriving During the Festive Season

Yu-Gi-Oh! Holiday Gifting Mastery: The Ultimate Guide for Fans and Newcomers Alike

Holiday Harmony: A Hydrocephalus Survival Guide for the Festive Season

Celestial Craft: The Witch's Almanac for 2025 – A Cosmic Guide to Manifestations, Moons, and Mystical Events

Doctor Who: The Toymaker's Winter Wonderland

Tulsa King Unveiled: A Thrilling Guide to Stallone's Mafia Masterpiece

Pendulum Craft: A Complete Guide to Crafting and Using Personalized Divination Tools

Nightmare Mansion: Santa's Eternal Eve

Starlight Noel: A Cosmic Journey through Christmas Mysteries

The Dark Architect: Unlocking the Blueprint of Existence

Surviving the Embrace: The Ultimate Guide to Encounters with The Hugging Molly

The Enchanted Codex: Secrets of the Craft for Witches, Wiccans, and Pagans

Harvest of Gratitude: A Complete Thanksgiving Guide

Yuletide Essentials: A Complete Guide to an Authentic and Magical Christmas

Celestial Smokes: A Cosmic Guide to Cigars and Astrology

Living in Balance: A Comprehensive Survival Guide to Thriving with Diabetes Insipidus

Cosmic Symbiosis: The Venom Zodiac Chronicles

The Cursed Paw of Ambition

Cosmic Symbiosis: The Astrological Venom Journal

Celestial Wonders Unfold: A Stargazer's Guide to the Cosmos (2024-2029)

The Ultimate Black Friday Prepper's Guide: Mastering Shopping Strategies and Savings

Cosmic Sales: The Astrological Guide to Black Friday Shopping

Legends of the Corn Mother and Other Harvest Myths

Whispers of the Harvest: The Corn Mother's Journal

The Evergreen Spellbook

The Doctor Meets the Boogeyman

The White Witch of Rose Hall's SpellBook

The Gingerbread Golem's Shadow: A Study in Sweet Darkness

The Gingerbread Golem Codex: An Academic Exploration of Sweet Myths

The Gingerbread Golem Grimoire: Sweet Magicks and Spells for the Festive Witch

The Curse of the Gingerbread Golem

10-minute Christmas Crafts for kids

Christmas Crisis Solutions: The Ultimate Last-Minute Survival Guide

Gingerbread Golem Recipes: Holiday Treats with a Magical Twist

The Infinite Key: Unlocking Mystical Secrets of the Ages

Enchanted Yule: A Wiccan and Pagan Guide to a Magical and Memorable Season

Dinosaurs of Power: Unlocking Ancient Magick

Astro-Dinos: The Cosmic Guide to Prehistoric Wisdom

Gallifrey's Yule Logs: A Festive Doctor Who Cookbook

The Dino Grimoire: Secrets of Prehistoric Magick

The Gift They Never Knew They Needed

The Gingerbread Golem's Culinary Alchemy: Enchanting Recipes for a Sweetly Dark Feast

A Time Lord Christmas: Holiday Adventures with the Doctor

Krampusproofing Your Home: Defensive Strategies for Yule

Silent Frights: A Collection of Christmas Creepypastas to Chill Your Bones

Santa Raptor's Jolly Carnage: A Dino-Claus Christmas Tale

Prehistoric Palettes: A Dino Wicca Coloring Journey

The Christmas Wishkeeper Chronicles

The Starlight Sleigh: A Holiday Journey

Elf Secrets: The True Magic of the North Pole

Candy Cane Conjurations

Cooking with Kids: Recipes Under 20 Minutes

Doctor Who: The TARDIS Confiscation

The Anxiety First Aid Kit: Quick Tools to Calm Your Mind

Frosty Whispers: A Winter's Tale

The Infinite Key: Unlocking the Secrets to Prosperity, Resilience, and Purpose

The Grasping Void: Why You'll Regret This Purchase

Astrology for Busy Bees: Star Signs Simplified

The Instant Focus Formula: Cut Through the Noise

The Secret Language of Colors: Unlocking the Emotional Codes

Sacred Fossil Chronicles: Blank Journal

The Christmas Cottage Miracle

Feeding Frenzy: Graboid-Inspired Recipes

Manifest in Minutes: The Quick Law of Attraction Guide

The Symbiote Chronicles: Doctor Who's Venomous Journey

Think Tiny, Grow Big: The Minimalist Mindset

The Energy Key: Unlocking Limitless Motivation

New Year, New Magic: Manifesting Your Best Year Yet

Unstoppable You: Mastering Confidence in Minutes

Infinite Energy: The Secret to Never Feeling Drained

Lightning Focus: Mastering the Art of Productivity in a Distracted World

Saturnalia Manifestation Magick: A Guide to Unlocking Abundance During the Solstice

Graboids and Garland: The Ultimate Tremors-Themed Christmas Guide

12 Nights of Holiday Magic

The Power of Pause: 60-Second Mindfulness Practices

The Quick Reset: How to Reclaim Your Life After Burnout

The Shadow Eater: A Tale of Despair and Survival

The Micro-Mastery Method: Transform Your Skills in Just Minutes a Day

Reclaiming Time: How to Live More by Doing Less
Chronovore: The Eternal Nexus
The Mind Reset: Unlocking Your Inner Peace in a Chaotic World
Confidence Code: Building Unshakable Self-Belief
Baby the Vampire Terrier
Baby the Vampire Terrier's Christmas Adventure
Celestial Streams: The Content Creator's Astrology Manual
The Wealth Whisperer: Unlocking Abundance with Everyday Actions
The Energy Equation: Maximize Your Output Without Burning Out
The Happiness Algorithm: Science-Backed Steps to Joyful Living
Stress-Free Success: Achieving Goals Without Anxiety
Mindful Wealth: The New Blueprint for Financial Freedom
The Festive Flavors of New Year: A Culinary Celebration
The Master's Gambit: Keys of Eternal Power
Shadowed Secrets: Groundhog Day Mysteries
Beneath the Burrow: Lessons from the Groundhog
Spring's Whispers: The Groundhog's Prediction
The Limitless Mindset: Unlock Your Untapped Potential
The Focus Funnel: How to Cut Through Chaos and Get Results
Bold Moves: Building Courage to Live on Your Terms
The Daily Shift: Simple Practices for Lasting Transformation
The Quarter-Life Reset: Thriving in Your 20s and 30s
The Art of Shadowplay: Building Your Own Personal Myth
The Eternal Loop: Finding Purpose in Repetition
Burrowing Wisdom: Life Lessons from the Groundhog
Shadow Work: A Groundhog Day Perspective
Love in Bloom: 5-Minute Romantic Gestures
The Shadowspell Codex: Secrets of Forbidden Magick
The Burnout Cure: Finding Balance in a Busy World
The Groundhog Prophecy: Unlocking Seasonal Secrets
Nog Tales: The Spirited History of Eggnog

Six More Weeks: Embracing Seasonal Transitions
The Lumivian Chronicles: Fragments of the Fifth Dimension
Money on Your Mind: A Beginner's Guide to Wealth
The Focus Fix: Breaking Through Distraction
January's Spirit Keepers: Mystical Protectors of the Cold
Creativity Unchained: Unlocking Your Wildest Ideas in 2025
Manifestation Mastery: 365 Days to Rewrite Your Reality
The Groundhog's Mirror: Reflecting on Change
The Weeping Angels' Christmas Curse
Burrowed in Time: A Groundhog Day Journey
Heartbeats: Poems to Share with Your Valentine
Dino Wicca: The Sacred Grimoire of Prehistoric Magick
Courage of the Pride: Finding Your Inner Roar
The Lion's Leap: Bold Moves for Big Results
Healthy Hustle: Achieving Without Overworking
Practical Manifesting: Turning Dreams into Reality in 2025
Jurassic Pharaohs: Unlocking the Magick of Ancient Egypt and Dino Wicca
The Happiness Equation: Small Changes for Big Joy
The Confidence Compass: Finding Your Inner Strength
Whispers in the Hollow: Tales of the Forgotten Beasts
Echoes from the Hollow: The Return of Forgotten Beasts
The Hollow Ascendant: The Rise of the Forgotten Beasts
The Relationship Reset: Building Better Connections
Mastering the Morning: How to Win the Day Before 8 AM
The Shadow's Dance: Groundhog Day Symbolism
Cupid's Kitchen: Quick Valentine's Day Recipes
Valentine's Day on a Budget: Love Without Breaking the Bank
Astrocraft: Aligning the Stars in the World of Minecraft
Forecasting Life: Groundhog Day Reflections
Bleeding Hearts: Twisted Tales of Valentine's Terror
Herbal Smoke Revolution: The Ultimate Guide to Nature's Cigarette Alternative

Winter's Wrath: The Complete Survival Blueprint for Extreme Freezes.

The Groundhog's Shadow: A Tale of Seasons

Burrowed Insights: Wisdom from the Groundhog

Sensual Strings: The Art of Erotic Bondage

Whispered Flames: Unlocking the Power of Fire Play

Forgotten Shadows: A Guide to Cryptids Lost to Time

Six Weeks of Secrets: Groundhog Day's Hidden Messages

Shadows and Cycles: Groundhog Day Reflections

The Art of Love Letters: Crafting the Perfect Message

Romantic Getaways at Home: Turning Your Space into Paradise

Purrfect Brews: A Cat Lover's Guide to Coffee and Companionship

The Groundhog's Wisdom: Timeless Lessons for Modern Life

The Shadow Oracle: Groundhog Day as a Predictor

Emerging from the Burrow: A Journey of Renewal

The Language of Love: Learning Your Partner's Love Style

Authorpreneur: The Ultimate Blueprint for Writing, Publishing, and Thriving as an Author

Weathering the Seasons: Groundhog Day Perspectives

Valentine's Day Magic: A Guide to Romantic Rituals

The Shadow Chronicles: Stories of Groundhog Day

Love and Laughter: Fun Games for Valentine's Day

AstroRealty: Unlocking the Stars for Property Success

The Groundhog's Path: A Guide to Seasonal Balance

Groundhog Day Diaries: Reflections in the Shadow

The Groundhog's Light: Illuminating the Path Ahead

Valentine's Traditions from Around the World

AI Wealth Revolution: Unlocking the Trillionaire Mindset

Love Rekindled: Reigniting Passion in Relationships

Single and Thriving: Self-Love on Valentine's Day

Emerald Legends: Mystical Tales of Ireland

Green Alchemy: Harnessing Nature's Magic
The Hearts of Horror: A Valentine's Day Nightmare
The Leprechaun's Guide to Wealth and Wisdom
Dancing with the Sidhe: Celebrating the Otherworld
Shamrocks and Shadows: Mysteries of the Green Isle
Emerald Energy: Harnessing Luck and Growth
The Gingerbread Golem's Valentine: A Sweetheart's Guide to Love and Enchantment
The Celtic Knot: Weaving Life and Destiny
Green Fire: Elemental Magic for St. Patrick's Day
Clover Chronicles: Finding Your Inner Luck
Ireland's Mystical Creatures: A Field Guide
Gingerbread Golem's Love Almanac
Prowl and Thrive: The Lion's Guide to Success
Love Alchemy: Transforming Your Life Through Heart Energy
WORLD DOMINATION: Woman's Rule 3:The New Life
The Midnight Rose: A Guide to Lunar Love Spells
The Forbidden Letters: Writing Your Own Love Prophecy
Luck and Lore: St. Patrick's Day for Modern Mystics
The Green Path: A Pagan Celebration of Renewal
The Dark Architect's Guide to Reprogramming Reality
Prankster's Paradise: A Guide to Harmless Hijinks
Manifest Your Reality: The Law of Attraction Simplified
The TARDIS Owner's Manual: Understanding the Doctor's Ship: *A complete guide to the TARDIS, its technology, secrets, and mysteries*
Starlit Romance: Astrology Secrets for Finding True Love
The Time Lord's Atlas: A Complete Guide to the Whoniverse: ***A breakdown of the locations, planets, and dimensions explored in Doctor Who***
Sweetheart Shadows: The Dark Side of Love and Attraction
February Fire: Reigniting Passion in Every Area of Life

The Self-Love Toolkit: 5 Ways to Embrace Who You Are
February Sparks: Ignite Your Dreams in 28 Days
March to Success: A 31-Day Action Blueprint
Ancient Paths: The 13 Sacred Principles of Dino Wicca
Echoes of Tomorrow: Navigating the AI Revolution
The Wellness Blueprint: Balancing Mind, Body, and Soul
Green Horizons: Sustainable Living for a Better Tomorrow
The AI Wealth Code: How to Make Millions with Automation
AI-Powered Creativity: Writing, Art, and Music for Profit
Extinction Rites: Rebirthing Your Soul Through Prehistoric Magick
Sacred Serpents tarot
Celestial Enchantment blank journal
Star Strains
Culinary Journeys: Exploring Global Flavors at Home
The Hollowvale Curse
The Hollowvale Harvest
The Egg of Transformation: Awakening Your Inner Power
Blooming Into Power: A Wiccan Guide to Spring Awakening
The Nightmare Nexus: The Third Doctor's Perilous Haunting
Digital Detox: Reclaiming Your Life in a Connected World
Ostara's Path: Walking the Spiral of Renewal
The Sacred Hare
Financial Freedom: Building Wealth in the Modern Age
Spring's Cauldron: Stirring the Waters of Change
The Hollowvale Pact
Quantum Consciousness: The Science of Reality Shifting
The Hollowvale Hunger
The Sacred Waters Within: A Witch's Guide to Hydrocephalus Magick
The Raven's Nest: Building a Life of Unshakable Stability
AI and the Human Mind: The Future of Intelligence
The Hollowvale Reckoning

Timeless Love: Building and Maintaining Lasting Relationships

The Raven's Roar: Unlocking Unstoppable Confidence

Raven Sight: Awakening Intuition and Inner Wisdom

The Butterfly Effect: Small Changes, Big Transformations

Taming the Boogeyman: How to Conquer Your Inner Fears

The Magick of Green: Awakening Earth's Energy in You

The Entrepreneurial Mindset: Secrets to Business Success

The Hollowvale End

The Shadow Luck Ritual: Reclaiming Power from Your Dark Side

Spring Magick for Beginners: A Simple Guide to Seasonal Energy Work

Doctor Who: The Hollowvale Conundrum

The March of Miracles: Unlocking Synchronicities in Spring

Unveiling the Cosmos: A Guide to Stargazing and Space Exploration

The Ultimate Guide to Surviving an Economic Collapse

The AI Gold Rush: How to Profit from the AI Revolution

Bastet's Shadow: The Hidden Power of Feline Magick

The Bastet Codex: Unlocking the Goddess's Magickal Secrets

Purring Spells: Harnessing Bastet's Healing Frequencies

Bastet's Nine Lives: Rebirth, Transformation, and Immortality Spells

Primal Currents: Hydrocephalus Magick in the Path of Dino Wicca

The Digital Gold Rush: Mastering E-Commerce and Online Sales

Future Shock: Adapting to the Next Decade of Change

The Quantum Mindset: Think Like a Billionaire

Sacred Motherhood: Awakening the Divine Feminine Within

The Mother's Spellbook: Enchantments for Love, Protection, and Prosperity

The Witch's Guide to Parenting: Raising Empowered and Intuitive Children

The Magick of Motherhood: Reclaiming Your Power Through Rituals

The Pagan Path to Self-Love: A Goddess's Guide to Worth and Confidence

Wild Woman Magick: Unleashing Your Primal Power

The Money Magnet Blueprint: Unlocking Unlimited Wealth

Biohacking 101: Unlock Your Body's Full Potential

The Wild Father: A Pagan Guide to Strength and Wisdom

The Sacred Masculine: Unlocking Your Inner Power

The Druid's Compass

The Warrior's Mindset

The Father's Fire

Odin's Path

Ancestral Bonds

The House That Whispers

The Magician's Code

The Wild Hunt

The Green Man's Path

The Altar of Success

The Shadow and the Sword

The High Priestess's Guide to Energy Healing

The Lunar Mother

The Sacred Self-Care Grimoire

The Womb Wisdom Codex

The Wheel of the Mother

The Witch's Guide to Manifestation

The Q2 Reset

The Ultimate Guide to AI-Powered Passive Income

Escape the 9-5

AI Feline Fortunes

The Tear-Stained Grimoire

Razorblade Runes
Cemetery Sirens
The Midnight Wristwatch
The Town That Forgets
AI Horror & Creepypasta
The Hollow Frequency
The Breach Echo
The Quiet Between Worlds
The Sigil of Tharan-Khul
Summon the Vault of Y'ha'ten
The Becoming Codex
The Profit of Az'ra-nar
The Drowned Logos
Echoes of the Eldritch Will
The Deep Ledger
Necronomicon of Networth
Covenant of the Wealthwyrm
The Whisperer's Manifesto
The Rites of Azh-K'luth
The Ark of the Crawling Coin
The Tithe of Shadows
Inkheart Abyss
The Timewinds of Y'ha-nthlei
The Spiral Labyrinth of Azag-Nirrh
The Gallifreyan Heresy of the Black Pharaoh
The Psalms of Nyog-Sotha
Black Rain Alchemy
The Infinite Maw
The Entropic Blueprint
The Oracle of Sh'guul
The Book of Breach
The Drowned Saint's Testament
Dreamcraft of the Sleeper God

The Silence Market
Cthonomics: The Dark Wealth Algorithm
Invocation of the Ten-Eyed King
Wealthbound to the Wyrm Below
Become the Unnameable
Codex of the Sovereign Flame
Rituals of Relentless Becoming
The Shadow Ascends
The Eyes Beneath You
The Will That Wakes Worlds
Silence Is a Weapon
The Mirror That Screams
The Whisper Between Moments
The Mind That Devours Fear
The Myth of the Finished Self
The Architect of Your Madness
The Voice You've Buried
The Discipline of Madness
Stormborn: Awakening Your Inner Tempest
The Mind That Ate Time
Unbind Your Becoming
The Pact You Owe Yourself
The Devourer's Diet
The Acid That Carves the Path
The Tower You Must Burn
The Breath Between Worlds
Speak Like the Deep
The Labyrinth Within
The Spine of the Sea God
Rejection Is a Portal
The Crown You Refused
The Scar Is the Spell
The Lightless Flame

The Habit of Becoming Horrific
ChickenJockey Chaos
The Gatekeeper Within
You Are Not Your Name
The Compass of the Mad
The Archive of Unsent Letters
What the Mirror Can't Show You
The Knife You Needed
Worship Nothing, Become Everything
The Other Voice
The Body the World Forgot
The Vein of the Void
The Black Bone Codex
The Puzzle of the Hidden Self (Millennium Puzzle)
The Eye That Sees the Lie *(Millennium Eye)*
The Ring of Return (Millennium Ring)
The Rod of Relentless Will ***(Millennium Rod)***
The Tally of the Soul (Millennium Tauk/Necklace)
The Key to the Locked Timeline (Millennium Key)
The Scale of Sacred Decisions (Millennium Scales)
Inferno Bites: The UnOfficial Minecraft Lava Cookbook
Rot in the Attic
Prana: The Hidden Force of Your Infinite Self
The Shadow Realm Within: Transforming Darkness Into Destiny
The Borderland Collapse
Claws of Protection: Bastet's Defensive Magick
Mr. Ring-a-Ding's Madness
Yugioh Astrology: Celestial Deckcraft and Duel Destiny (2026–2027 Edition)
The Seal You Signed: Unlocking the Power You Once Feared
The Puzzle of Infinite Minds: Unlocking the Mentalism Hidden Within

The Eye That Mirrors the All: Secrets of Inner Reflection
Doctor Who: The Toymaker's Broadcast
The Rod of Eternal Flow: Commanding the Currents of Vibration
Golden Eyes of Bastet: Enhancing Psychic Vision
The Key of Dual Forces: Balance Within the Polarity
The Scales of Living Rhythm: Timing the Dance of Life
The Necklace of Hidden Cause: Weaving the Webs of Fate
The Ring of Secret Masters: Rising Through the All Within All
Daggers of the Dying Deep
Bastet's Wealth and Fortune Magick: Prosperity Rituals of the Goddess
The Tide that Speaks
The Scrolls of Petosiris: 13 Rituals from the Feathered Eye
Petosiris and the Living Plague of Osirion
Feline Fire: Bastet's Passion and Love Magick
The Star Altar of Petosiris
Bastet's Whiskers: Supernatural Sensory Magick
The Bastet Grimoire
Feeding the Shadows
The Mouthless Prayer
The Spiral Wound
Becoming the Ibis: Lessons from Petosiris's Mind
The Crimson Coven: Cola Magick for Sweet Dominion
Sacred Cat's Paw
The Soda Zodiac: A Flavor for Every Sign
Covenant of the Crawling Flame
The Ink of Ish'Zur
Frothroot: The Thirst That Ate the World
The Golden Glyphs of Prosperity
The Etherbind Codex
Echoes of the Resistance: Reclaiming the You That Survived

Harnessed Minds: Breaking Free from Mental Control
The Eyes in the Smoke
Rootwake: The Carbon Covenant
Skitter Logic: Unlearning the Fear That Built You
Doctor Who: The World That Froths
Rootwake: The Fizz That Rewrites Flesh
Rootwake: Frothfather of the World
The Holly Pact: Blood Beneath the Mistletoe
The 2nd Mass Principle: Building Unbreakable Tribes
Web of Wits: A Survival Guide to Encounters with Anasi the Spider (Aunt Nancy)
The Hexbreaking Handbook: Effective Spells to Remove Curses
Pop Alchemy: Transform Your Life One Sip at a Time
The Mason Code: Leading in Unleadable Times
Petosiris and the Fifth Chamber of Thoth
The Ether Seed Within
The Parent of Tomorrow
Petosiris's Pyramid of Perpetual Wealth
Unlearn the World
Grimoire of the Hollow Tongue
Zodiac Weeds: Finding Your Strain Through the Stars
Aquarius Rises in the Bank
The Sugar God's Smile
The Skinclock Reversal: Biohacking the Face of Time
Debtburn: How to Obliterate What You Owe Forever
The Ice Cream Oracle: What Your Cone Says About Your Future
Silence Is Sovereignty: The Power of Being Unreadable
The Wind That Whispers Through Stone
Path of the Four Directions
Doctor Who: The Maestro's Symphony of Endings
Oxygen Grail: Breathing to Undo the Clock

Zodiacal Collapse: When Stars Devour Time
Teachings from the Red Sand Silence
Doctor Who: Omega – The Broken Equation
Memory Wipe Your Past: Start Over Like a MiB
Mitochondria Prime: Ignite the Core of Youth
A Nest of Roaches
Grub from the Galaxy: MiB Recipes You'll Never Forget
Whiskers of Power: Bastet's Guide to Inner Sovereignty
The Gift Must Cost Them: Negotiation Through Unequal Exchange
The Worm Guys' Wealth Code: Hustle Like an Alien
Bug Out: The Edgar Method for Ruthless Goal Setting
Weaving Life with Spiderwoman's Pattern
Doctor Who: The Rani's Renaissance
How to Get a Job (If You're a Puppygirl)
Speak Through Others: The Art of Proxy Power
T-Rex Your Trauma: Reclaim the Power of Your Primal Self
The Black Briefcase: How MiB Stay Wealthy in Silence
The Thirst Beyond Reason: Understanding Diabetes Insipidus From the Inside Out
Backwoods Witchcraft for Billionaires: The Pagan Path from Dirt Roads to Gold Roads
The Moonshine Grimoire: Fermented Spells for Abundance
The Nameless Geometry
The Wraith's Mixtape: Spellcasting with Songs of Sorrow
The Gallifreyan Gentleman: Silent Wealth, Sonic Confidence, and the Doctor's Code of Living
Sugar Water Confidence
Dino Totems: Spirit Guides from Earth's First Gods
Pumpkin Sigils & Ritual Smoke
The Hózhó Compass
The Distortus Discipline – Order from Inner Mutation
Witchcraft for the Cold-Blooded Soul

Moonlight Over the Blessingway
Water, Interrupted: When the Body Forgets How to Hold On
Deformed but Divine: Embracing Your Asymmetry
Hexes in the Henhouse: The Farm Witch's Guide to Power
The Reversed Flame: A Grimoire of Inverted Power
Salt, Cells, and Sanity: Reclaiming Balance with Diabetes Insipidus
King of the Broken: Crowning the Flawed Self
Moonlight Scars: Emo Moon Magick and the Art of Lunar Sorrow
Noose Spells: Magick of the Hanging Rope
The Goth Cathedral: Rituals of the Broken and Beautiful
The Cretaceous Codex: Dino Spirits and Fossil Magick
The Turkey Bones Ritual
Nine Lives of Manifestation: Unlocking Bastet's Reality Codes
Chaos Muscles: Building Strength from Twisted Pain
Emo Blood Magick: The Veins of Power
The 3AM Flood: Nighttime Urination, Sleep Loss, and the DI Spiral
The Silence Between the Stars
The Lemon Method: Sour Your Way to Success
Starlit Sovereign
The Rite of Twelve Gates: Walking the Gates of the Duat.
Cornbread and Conjure: Recipes for Riches and Rootwork
The Black Rose Rituals: Emo Love Spells and Obsession Magick
The Eternal Goodbye: Death Magick and Rebirth Rituals
Sinkrot: The Drain That Remembers
The Hybrid Mindset: Thinking Beyond Evolution
Bone Dry: Navigating Dehydration Before It Breaks You
Wreathcraft: Winter Sigils and Yuletide Spells
The Rite of Twelve Mouths

S'mores of the Damned: Haunted Recipes for Halloween Night

Rethink the Drink: A Beverage Survival Guide for DI Warriors

The Shadow Chord: Guitar Magick and Sonic

Malformed Yet Majestic: Leading When You Feel Wrong Inside

The Cursed Diary: Ink-Stained Spells of the Emo Soul

Anxiety Off Switch: Emergency Reset for a Fried Nervous System

The Energy Heist: How to Take Back Your Life from Drainers

Beyond the Bathroom: Rebuilding Your Social Life With DI

Coyote's Gift for Decision Makers

Ghoul-Goo: Spooky S'mores You'll Die For

Echoes in the Mirror: Scrying and Self-Destruction Magick

Thread and Thorn: Stitching Spells from Rural Cloth

The Mogwai Mind: Building Untouchable Wealth from Small Ideas

Be Your Own Guide: Trust Your Inner Compass

Hormones in Chaos: The Endocrine Puzzle of Diabetes Insipidus

ChronoCleanse: Detox Your Biological Timeline

The Limb You Hide Is the One That Saves You

Leaves, Bones, and Whisper Spells

Get Some Tarot cards: https://www.makeplayingcards.com/sell/apophis-occult-shop

Get some shirts: https://www.bonfire.com/store/apophis-shirt-emporium/

<u>Instagrams:</u>
@apophis_enterprises,
@apophisbookemporium,
@apophisscardshop
Twitter: @apophisenterpr1
Tiktok:@apophisenterprise
Youtube: @sg1fan23477
Hive: @sg1fan23477
CheeLee: @SG1fan23477

Podcast: Apophis Chat Zone: https://open.spotify.com/show/5zXbrCLEV2xzCp8ybrfHsk?si=fb4d4fdbdce44dec

Newsletter: https://apophiss-newsletter-27c897.beehiiv.com/

If you want to support me or see posts of other projects that I have come over to: **buymeacoffee.com/mpetchinskg**

I post there daily several times a day

Get your Dinowicca or Christmas themed digital products, especially Santa Raptor songs and other musics. Here: **https://sg1fan23477.gumroad.com**

Apophis Yuletide Digital has not only digital Christmas items, but it will have all things with Dinowicca as well as other Digital products.

www.ingramcontent.com/pod-product-compliance
Lightning Source LLC
LaVergne TN
LVHW022220200926
848481LV00006B/2051